DOING REAL-LIFE CHANGE IN CHILDREN'S SOCIAL CARE

Embedded Research in Practice

Jenny Lloyd and Rachael Owens

First published in Great Britain in 2025 by

Policy Press, an imprint of
Bristol University Press
University of Bristol
1–9 Old Park Hill
Bristol
BS2 8BB
UK
t: +44 (0)117 374 6645
e: bup-info@bristol.ac.uk

Details of international sales and distribution partners are available at
policy.bristoluniversitypress.co.uk

© Bristol University Press 2025

British Library Cataloguing in Publication Data
A catalogue record for this book is available from the British Library

ISBN 978-1-4473-7238-7 paperback
ISBN 978-1-4473-7239-4 ePub
ISBN 978-1-4473-7240-0 ePdf

The right of Jenny Lloyd and Rachael Owens to be identified as authors of this work has been asserted by them in accordance with the Copyright, Designs and Patents Act 1988.

All rights reserved: no part of this publication may be reproduced, stored in a retrieval system, or transmitted in any form or by any means, electronic, mechanical, photocopying, recording, or otherwise without the prior permission of Bristol University Press.

Every reasonable effort has been made to obtain permission to reproduce copyrighted material. If, however, anyone knows of an oversight, please contact the publisher.

The statements and opinions contained within this publication are solely those of the authors and not of the University of Bristol or Bristol University Press. The University of Bristol and Bristol University Press disclaim responsibility for any injury to persons or property resulting from any material published in this publication.

Bristol University Press and Policy Press work to counter discrimination on grounds of gender, race, disability, age and sexuality.

Cover design: Liam Roberts
Front cover image: Getty/CSA-Printstock

We dedicate this book to the researcher and practitioner tasked with system change but not sure where to start. For the person with their head in their hands thinking: 'What is it I'm meant to do?' 'Where do I begin?' 'What do I know?' We hope this book can show you what is possible and what you can do.

Contents

List of figures, tables and boxes vii
List of exercises viii
About the authors ix
Acknowledgements x

1 Introduction 1

PART I Methods for understanding and changing children's social care systems 19

2 Embedded methods for learning how the system works 22

3 Methods for actively engaging with the system 46

4 Developing a plan and making changes 64

PART II Working with relationships, emotion and culture to change children's social care systems 87

5 Emotional containment and vulnerability in the change process 91

6 A relational approach to cultural change 107

7 Giving feedback on 'bad practice' 123

PART III Theories and learning from doing system change in children's social care 143

8 Reasons to be hopeful 145

| 9 | How theories can help us change systems | 160 |
| 10 | Conclusion | 174 |

| References | 187 |
| Index | 200 |

List of figures, tables and boxes

Figures

2.1	The child and family social care system, annotated with methods	27
3.1	Case file review system questions	54
7.1	The social discipline window	134
9.1	Multisystems in embedded research	170

Tables

3.1	Power-sharing opportunities	58
4.1	Modified version of a 'red, amber, green' rating table	69
4.2	System change plans	76

Boxes

4.1	Contextual Safeguarding pilots	78
4.2	Contextual Safeguarding pilot questions	80

List of exercises

2.1	Mapping	27
2.2	Aims	28
2.3	Making an observation template	33
3.1	Case file review	55
3.2	Understanding culture	56
4.1	Analytical framework	70
5.1	Getting beneath the surface	96
5.2	Finding out who you know	99
6.1	Growing the culture we want	112
6.2	Relationships of influence	115

About the authors

Jenny Lloyd is Associate Professor in the Department of Sociology at Durham University. In her work in the Contextual Safeguarding team, her research focuses on harm to young people during adolescence. Jenny cares passionately about working with practitioners to improve system responses. As an embedded researcher, she works within child protection services to improve responses to harm, including serious youth violence, child criminal exploitation and child sexual abuse. Jenny spends most of her time outside of work getting excited about new hobbies and pursuits.

Rachael Owens is Assistant Professor in the Department of Sociology at Durham University. Rachael began her career in the arts before transitioning to social work and social care, where she spent over two decades years working alongside parents, young people and families. During this time, she developed her interest and skills in reflective practice and relationship-based approaches. Her research in Contextual Safeguarding explores how to create social care practices that are ecological, grounded in an ethics of care and attentive to the emotional realities of life. She loves poetry, moving, singing, being outdoors and swimming, preferably all together.

Acknowledgements

We would like to express our deepest gratitude and respect to the young people, parents and carers who have been the focus and guiding motivation for the work described in this book. We hope that it contributes to systems that elevate your rights, create safety, and listen, and respond, to your needs.

To the sites and practitioners that partnered with us in the development of the Scale-Up project, we thank you for your trust, openness, determination, vulnerability and honesty. We have learned so much from you. The way you responded to the invitation to change almost everything about adolescent safeguarding is awe-inspiring. You are the bedrock of this work.

Our heartfelt thanks go to our incredible colleagues at both the University of Bedfordshire and Durham University. This book would not have been possible without the dedication, support and general brilliance of the Scale-Up team: Carly Adams Elias, Lisa Bostock, Vanessa Bradbury-Leather, Caroline Cresswell, Clive Diaz, Carlene Firmin, Gayanthi Hapuarachchi, Katie Latimer, Molly Manister, Hannah Millar, Lisa Thornhill and Joanne Walker. You have shared the highs and the lows of the work described in this book, and your contributions enriched our working lives and the pages of this book. We have been so lucky to have been able to share with you the many moments of joy and laughter, but also sadness and loss.

We are extremely fortunate, in an academic environment that can feel anything but kind, to have worked with the wider Contextual Safeguarding team throughout the period of this project. As well as the people mentioned already, this includes Rebecca Brown, Delphine Peace and Lauren Wroe.

We especially want to acknowledge Carlene Firmin. Not only did you develop and guide many of the methods and approaches that we outline in this book, but also you have been an incredible

Acknowledgements

and generous mentor and support to us. You saw something in us as researchers and women that you believed in, and through this, you have helped us to believe it too. We have been lucky to work together to develop change we believe in – this book would not have been possible without you.

Finally, we are grateful to our families for their love, support and endless cups of tea.

1

Introduction

Introduction

One day, in an online research team meeting, we were each giving an update on the children's social care services we'd recently visited. One researcher, when it was her turn, softly and with a heaviness not usual for the meeting told us that over the weekend a child in one of 'our' sites had died. Following their death, unrest had broken out in the area, as the young people and the community tried to make sense of what was happening. The researcher told us that when she returned to work on Monday, she saw that one of the professionals in that site had tried to contact her via email and telephone. We imagined they had wanted to contact her out of desperation, due to the events that were unfolding. But neither the researcher nor the team had been available. We, being academics, keep 'normal' office hours, and so we were unreachable.

This hit us hard. We felt sad and guilty. Perhaps to defend ourselves against these feelings, we wondered why they had contacted us? What did they think we could offer? We were just researchers after all! Later we learnt that it was to see if the researcher could join a large community meeting to talk about what had happened and to create a plan to support the young people locally. But in the moment, we were brought into the stark reality of what it's like to work in systems that are regularly managing and responding to the worst thing that can happen – a child's death. Hanging over us in that meeting was the horror of what had happened and the reality that we had an agenda to get through. But how do you move on to talk about project plans when someone has just told you that a child has died, and when you know that your 'research participants' – people you know and care about – are suffering? As we sat there quietly, Rachael offered to read a poem: 'Musée des Beaux Arts' by W.H. Auden (1938). The poem – which we recommend you look up, if possible, before reading further – describes a painting called *Landscape with the Fall of Icarus*, attributed to the Dutch painter Peter Bruegel the Elder (circa 1555). Although this might seem like a strange segue, as she read, we began to see the connection. Auden, looking at the painting, notices the absurdity and incongruity of one of life's paradoxes – that someone can be in the throes of terrible suffering (like Icarus, a boy falling from the sky) while at the exact same time mundane, ordinary moments also take place (a person opens a window, a horse scratches an itch). The poem helps us to look at how these very contrasting moments permanently and repeatedly coexist.

We'd been working with five children's social care sites for over a year. But on this day, we saw in a new way the paradoxes and complexities inherent in the relationships and roles we were creating. We came face to face with what it means to work in the 'real life' of children's social care systems – to be involved but also to be separate. Being the sort of researchers who embed themselves with the people they are researching isn't about climbing down from our ivory towers to trudge in the swampy lowlands of practice (Schön 1983). It's about becoming entwined with the incredible relational networks that shape and hold human systems together. Yes, it was our job to map and document 'evidence' about the systems we were working within. Yes, it was our job to formulate plans that would lead to change. But this was all happening with real people, real lives. Sometimes this meant that as we were opening a new tab on a spreadsheet or opening up a project plan, real tragedy was taking place alongside ordinary life, and we needed to find a way to hold these two things together.

In this book, we present the tools we have developed for doing embedded research alongside *a way* of doing it that connects with the realities of working with real people. The key message of this book is that you need robust frameworks and methods to help you understand systems and make changes, but these are not enough on their own. If we are to create deep and effective change, we also need to honour, value and respect the place of relationships, emotions and culture within systems. This is how we can do work that centers peoples' humanity.

What is real-life change?

This book is about 'real-life' change because it is grounded in the realities of what it is like to do research in real organisations with real people and real-life issues. We bring sociological approaches to understanding social systems (Bronfenbrenner 1979; Bourdieu 1984) together with psychosocial theories that allow us to enquire about what's 'beneath the surface' (Clarke and Hoggett 2019), within the relational and emotional terrain of organisational change. We believe that integrating sociological and psychosocial interpretations of the world gives our work a real-life richness. On the one hand, it allows us to acknowledge the external world, where there is structural inequality that we must challenge. And on the other, we can also pay attention to the 'internal' world, where feelings like anxiety and defensiveness can collectively influence systems in ways that, without this perspective, could be hard to fathom (Menzies Lyth 1960).

To give a hypothetical example, let's imagine that we are working with an organisation that wants to create better responses to children who have been hurt by weapons in their community. Through our embedded research, young people tell us about their experiences of racism (a form of structural harm) by adults, including the police. We also find that in social care, there are subtle differences about how Black young people are spoken about and responded to. These are forms of structural and systemic harm in the 'external world' that we can unearth using ecological and sociological approaches and methods. But when we take these findings to the organisation we are working with, individual staff act defensively. They ask us if we can really 'back that up', and they ask us not to use the word racism. Their 'inner world' feelings, anxieties and emotions significantly sway our work, making progress, and system change, difficult. These 'internal world' aspects of the work are much harder to capture. We learn that it is not just about understanding the staff members' feelings, but about finding ways to navigate relationships with them to be able to progress.

Psychosocial approaches foreground relationships and relationality (Ruch et al 2018). Within this perspective, relationships do not just offer a bridge that enables us to pass on new information, they also provide an embodied and experiential way of integrating new ways of seeing and being in the world. So to work with this organisation, we need to develop relationships that allow us to talk about the difficult things we observe and draw on these relationships to make change. We explore in this book how such a complex task can be supported by drawing on traditional embedded research approaches with both a sociological and relational sensibility, to reflect a more complex reality. The theoretical implications of this fusion are unpacked in Chapter 9.

What is embedded research?

Embedded research is a way of a doing research (or a 'methodology') that involves people with an explicit research role learning about an organisation by getting involved in the day-to-day life of the place they are studying, working in partnership with the people who live or work there. Embedded researchers are legitimised by the organisation as members of staff or by a status that facilitates them collecting data as part of a shared agreement with the organisation (McGinity and Salokangas 2014). A key element of embedded research that sets it apart from other ethnographic approaches which also involve spending 'ordinary' time with research participants (Hammersley 2006) is the role of collaboration to co-produce and implement changes (Cheetham et al 2018). As well as being focused on shared plans, embedded research is action orientated. Ultimately, those using the method – researchers – and those that have systems to change – people in organisations – work together to make changes that actually improve the organisation and the research knowledge in that area.

There are of course challenges with this methodology. Embedded researchers have highlighted the complexities of navigating relationships (Duggan 2014; Vindrola-Padros et al 2017), ethics (Lloyd 2021), different personalities (Lewis and Russell 2011) and varied organisational cultures (Wong 2009) to name but a few. Yet, in addition to these challenges, there are many benefits, including being able to practically apply the research findings (Baars 2014), having research that is relevant to the organisational context (Ghaffar et al 2017) and increasing practitioner capacity (Westlake et al 2020). Ultimately, though, unlike many research approaches, embedded research allows research findings to have an impact on practice, and quickly.

The extent to which researchers are 'embedded' in organisations can vary significantly. Ask yourself: if I didn't turn up at the organisation one day, would anyone notice? In some of our projects, people would certainly have noticed if we weren't there, but this was not the case in most instances. Whether you are confidently flying the flag as an embedded researcher, proudly wearing your organisational lanyard and wishing security staff 'good morning' by name each day or sheepishly turning up and never quite sure where to sit, don't worry. It is possible to use the methods in this book whatever your level of 'embeddedness'. For us, embedded research is less about 'being there' all the time (although this would certainly facilitate the method) and more about building the right sort of relationships that enable good enough access, meaningful collaboration and positive impact. You'll need three things to be in place to work in this way. First, ensure you are working collaboratively *with* organisations to a shared plan for research and implementation (El-Hoss et al 2024). Second, you need practical and relational access to the people and 'data' that the organisation holds – including sign-off from senior staff, log-in details, security clearance and logistical knowledge of how to 'get in' (that might be quite literal). This access is not to be taken lightly; a significant privilege and benefit of embedded research is the level of access to sensitive information it's possible to gain – the sort of things 'outsiders' rarely see. Finally, the method relies extensively on your ability to form relationships (see Part II). So, whether or not staff miss you at the 11 o'clock coffee break, it is essential that you find ways to connect with others throughout the process.

Who is this book for?

This book is aimed at two broad groups. The first group is made up of other researchers, such as doctoral students, academics or those working in charities or think tanks who are interested in *doing* research with services to make change. The second group is made up of professionals working in human services who are creating change in their organisation. We refer to this group as 'local leaders' or 'local teams'. Because we are drawing on our experience as researchers, we use the term 'researcher' to describe the person going into an organisation, learning about how it works and co-creating a plan to create change. However, you don't have to be a researcher, and certainly not an academic one, to use this book.

When it comes to *what* system and *what* change you want to make, we see three reasons for reading this book. First, as it is based on research about Contextual Safeguarding system change, it will be useful for those interested in creating Contextual Safeguarding systems or adolescent safeguarding approaches. Second, the methods could be used by those interested in applying embedded methods and system change in children's social care, beyond Contextual Safeguarding. Finally, the book also has utility for those interested generally in embedded approaches to change systems. While some methods are specific to children's social care, we have written each part, and included relevant exercises, to allow for broad application to human services.

Ultimately, if you have been tasked with creating system change – be that in children's social care or in wider human services – this book is for you. It's for the researcher or professional sitting at their desk, head in hands, wondering 'what am I meant to do?' For the person with a lovely plan but no idea how to start, or the one who wants to 'collect data' but keeps getting pulled into the 'small talk', 'gossip' and 'off the record' discussions with no idea how to use this information meaningfully, this book will support you to collect the 'evidence' you need while valuing the relationships that bind everything together. We – and this book – are here to help you on the journey of embedded research and system change.

What is this book about?

The book is in three parts. Part I is about methods (or tools) for changing children's social care systems. We describe how you can understand the system using methods like case file review, meeting observations and other ethnographic research tools. We include illustrative examples from our work and supportive exercises for you to follow. Part I also describes how you can analyse your data, turning it into a plan that leads to actual changes in systems. We explain our analytical framework, help you build your own and discuss how to do these things in partnership with organisations.

Part II is about the networks that sustain system change, which are made up of relationships, culture, and emotions. We dig down into these to explore how we can work with the 'messier', less predictable parts of system change. The chapters in this part draw on our experiences to consider how relationships help create cultural change, the different roles that people occupy within embedded research and ways to navigate problematic practice. By combining sociological and psychosocial approaches, we show how we coped with the complexity and demands of this work by giving space for these more 'hidden' – but no less lively – aspects of systems.

In Part III, we take a step back and explore the wider meaning and implications of doing embedded research in the way we've described. We explain, and give examples of, the kinds of system changes we've seen take place through our work to help you develop a realistic but hopeful vision for what you can also achieve. This part also explores how we have drawn on, and integrated, several theoretical concepts to help us in our work. In this way, we have arrived at a multisystemic theoretical framework that allows us to do work which is holistic and reflective of real life.

In each part of the book, we share some creative writing that we produced during the research and process of writing the book. We found that writing about the methods and data in this way gave us access to the emotional implications of our work, which were not always surfaced through our more 'academic' analysis. We have included our 'first attempts' and relatively unedited versions to encourage you to do the same. They aren't intended to be great works of art, but rather opportunities to play with and think about data in different ways.

The book also references an online toolkit, which you can find on the Contextual Safeguarding website (www.contextualsafeguarding.org.uk) in the section 'Real-life book'. The toolkit contains the resources in this book – the real-life examples of the methods we have used – and shows you how we turn research into resources that benefit practice.

What is this book not about?

This book is not a comprehensive breakdown of every possible method that could be employed in embedded research. Instead, you'll find an explanation of our key methods and a deep dive into tools and approaches that you might be less familiar with. Although we use them in our work, we haven't covered methods like interviews and focus groups, as these have been extensively written about elsewhere (for example, Cyr 2016; Roulston and Choi 2018).

For different reasons, this book does not give a detailed outline of the participation of, or consultation with, 'service users' – that is, the people for whom welfare services exist, who in our case are young people and parents/carers. The Scale-Up project (described later) included a research strand on engaging young people and parents/carers. This involved partnering with local voluntary and community sector organisations that were already working with young people impacted by extra-familial harm who had experience of children's services. Through working with these organisations, researchers in the team (but not the authors of this book) worked with young people to learn about and explore their views on the types of system change we were proposing (Millar et al 2023). These findings were then integrated into the system changes that each site developed.

System change is a broad field, but it is fair to say that those making changes to children's social care systems have often neglected to involve the very people that they impact the most – children, young people and their families – as part of the change process (Jobe and Gorin 2013; Warrington and Larkins 2019). Thankfully, the tide is turning and participation and engagement with young people is beginning to be recognised as essential to this work (Department for Education 2023). Participation and engagement with young people has significantly shaped the ethics and methods we have used to approach embedded research and system change. However, it would be disingenuous to overstate the participatory elements of the system change we focus on in this book. In a perfect world, the embedded elements of research and system change would run together with the participatory elements, each symbiotically influencing the other. However, this was not the case. Anyone who has done participatory research with young people – and, in our case, young people impacted by extra-familial harm – will know how time-consuming and difficult this work can be (Kim 2016). To do it justice, we recommend engaging with the brilliant resources and literature that exist on participation and system change (Warrington et al 2016). We have also developed a range of our own resources on this, which are freely accessible online via the 'Scale-Up toolkit' on the Contextual Safeguarding website. In this book, we focus most on the *embedded* elements of the work, so it's a book about working *with* professionals *in* children's social care systems, as opposed to *with* young people *about* social care systems. Doing the latter is incredibly important, but it was not the substantive focus of the research methodology described in this book.

This book is also not specifically about research ethics and the ethical dilemmas and implications of the approach and methods, though where specific ethical questions emerge about the methods, these are discussed. However, we do not see ethics as an 'add-on'. Questions of ethics and the principles of rigorous, fair inquiry flow through our research design. We have very much been led and influenced by the research institutes that we have worked within. The Safer Young Lives centre at the University of Bedfordshire, where Contextual Safeguarding was first developed, helped guide much of our approach and thinking (Safer Young Lives 2024).

Finally, this book is not a 'how to' guide to Contextual Safeguarding. All the specific learning from our system change projects have been developed into resources that are available on the Contextual Safeguarding website. The Scale-Up toolkit includes over 150 resources that provide real-life examples and frameworks to help people make changes similar to the ones we made. To ensure that this book has application beyond the area of extra-familial harm, we draw on examples from Contextual Safeguarding, but do so illustratively.

What is Contextual Safeguarding?

Having said that this book isn't about how to do Contextual Safeguarding, it is still useful to give a short overview of the approach and its history to contextualise the work we draw on in this book. Contextual Safeguarding is about creating safeguarding systems that can address the harm young people encounter in their communities. It is an approach that considers the role that social, cultural and geographical contexts play in the harm that happens to young people. For example, if a child is the victim of knife violence on the street outside their school, a Contextual Safeguarding approach would think about what could be done to make both the child and the street safer. If this took place in an area where there was a Contextual Safeguarding approach, professionals would think about why the young person who caused the harm felt the need to carry a knife. For example, was there a lack of protective adults? Did they feel unsafe, and why? Professionals would consider if other incidents had happened and what could be done to make the street safer for all the young people who spent time there. They would also engage the school and other partners to create a plan for change.

Contextual Safeguarding was developed by Professor Carlene Firmin. She reviewed nine cases of peer-on-peer violence in the United Kingdom (UK) and found that despite the young people encountering significant harm, there either wasn't a children's social care response to the harm or the response to the young people was not appropriate to address their welfare needs (Firmin 2015). This is because in the UK, the traditional children's social care system was not designed to address harm outside families. These forms of interpersonal violence and abuse, referred to as 'extra-familial harm', include children experiencing violence on the street, experiencing sexual exploitation in groups and being exploited to traffic drugs. Although these forms of harm often involve 'significant harm' – this is the legal test outlined in English law (in the Children Act 1989) that determines if a child should receive a child protection response – the system was not designed to address them. In practice, children's social care responses to abuse and harm is focused on parenting – whether parents are hurting children or not doing enough to protect them from harm. However, when children are harmed outside their homes, parents often have very little influence over what happens. Carlene identified how factors beyond parents – for example, a young person's peer group or the places where the harm happened – contributed significantly to enabling or preventing harm. In doing so, she called for 'rewriting the rules of child protection' to 'create a system capable of [tackling] the norms of schools, neighbourhood and peer contexts in which abuse has occurred [and] tackl[ing] the rules of child protection systems that themselves have focused on intervention with families as the primary route for protection in the face of abuse' (Firmin 2020, p 8).

In 2015, Carlene published her thesis and the theory of Contextual Safeguarding was born (Firmin 2015). In 2018, she secured funding from the UK Department for Education to work in collaboration with the London Borough of Hackney on a project focused on turning the theory into practice by building the first Contextual Safeguarding system in children's social care. Jenny worked on the project as a member of the Contextual Safeguarding research programme. Rachael joined the project as a social work manager employed by Hackney. In 2019, funding was secured to test further system change in five children's social care departments in England and Wales as part of the Scale-Up project. A further four London sites were added in 2020.

Since 2015, Contextual Safeguarding has entered statutory safeguarding guidance in England, Scotland and Wales (HM Government 2018; Welsh Government 2020; Scottish Government 2021). The Contextual Safeguarding research team have now formally tested the approach in ten children's social care departments, and, at the time of writing, over 80 social care departments and safeguarding agencies in the UK have committed to taking a Contextual Safeguarding approach. A large focus of this commitment is on changing social care systems. We – Jenny and Rachael – worked on these projects as operational leads and embedded researchers in the sites. The learning from the Scale-Up project forms the basis of this book.

Why did the system need to change?

We have touched briefly on some of the challenges of the traditional child safeguarding response to children harmed outside their families. From the early 2000s, public interest in some of the harms facing children outside their families started to increase the pressure on policy makers and safeguarding professionals to alter how these forms of harm were addressed (Jay 2014). For example, there was growing recognition of the need to understand child sexual exploitation as a form of abuse rather than viewing children as 'prostituting' themselves (Melrose 2013). Similar public and policy shifts were seen a decade later with growing awareness of the harm children faced when being exploited to traffic drugs via 'county lines' or experiencing other forms of criminal exploitation (Cockbain and Olver 2019). This was supported by a policy environment that called for a welfare-based response, led by children's social care, to these forms of extra-familial harm, whereas previously responses had been led by youth justice or there was no response at all (HM Government 2018; Firmin, Lefevre et al 2022).

Despite this favourable policy environment, young people, their families, researchers and professionals were highlighting the inadequacies of the systems within which they were now being asked to create new responses (Beckett et al 2013; Warrington et al 2016; Firmin 2017a). In short, it was not enough to say that children experiencing these forms of harm *should* receive a welfare response when the system for providing such a response was not fit for the task of addressing harm outside families. This is because, even when children experienced forms of harm that were extremely significant, these did not always meet the 'threshold' for children's social care (Lloyd and Firmin 2020). To be blunt, children were dying at the hands of their peers, being raped by adults for money and being sent across the country on their own to sell drugs, but these forms of harm were often not seen to meet the threshold for a social care response. This is because the children's social care system was not designed to respond to these forms of harm. Rather, the system was focused either on the 'capacity' of parents to keep their young people safe or on altering the behaviour of young people – and, in so doing, holding them responsible for things beyond their control (Hallett 2015; Thornhill 2023). A contextual view of young people's agency was not recognised and instead young people were viewed in simplistic ways, either as 'choosing' to be harmed (Pearce 2013)

Introduction

or as harmful 'perpetrators'. In response to these challenges, the Contextual Safeguarding framework offered a way to redesign the whole system of children's social care. But this was no easy task.

The Contextual Safeguarding framework and values

In 2017, Carlene Firmin developed the underpinning features of the Contextual Safeguarding system. These are expressed as four domains (Firmin 2017b):

1. Target the social conditions of abuse by preventing, identifying, assessing and intervening within those contexts. If the harm was in a park, a school or online, the assessment and response should address the dynamics, features and relationships of that context.
2. Incorporate extra-familial contexts into child protection frameworks, ensuring that responses to these forms of harm draw on welfare approaches rather than solely crime prevention.
3. Develop partnerships with the sectors and individuals who have influence in, and responsibility for, those contexts. That might be teachers in a school, people in local businesses or others who have influence over that context.
4. Measure outcomes of success in relation to contextual as well as individual change.

Five values were added to the framework following the collective work of the Contextual Safeguarding programme (Wroe 2020) – Contextual Safeguarding systems need to be:

- **collaborative** – they should involve collaboration with professionals, children and young people, families and communities to inform decisions about safety.
- **ecological** – they should consider the links between the spaces where young people experience harm and how these are shaped by inequalities.
- **rights based** – they should be rooted in children's and human rights.
- **strengths based** – they should build on the strengths of individuals and communities to achieve change.

- **evidence informed** – they should produce research that is grounded in the reality of how life happens and propose solutions informed by lived experience.

When we, the Contextual Safeguarding team, embarked on creating system change using embedded research methods, it was these four domains and five values that guided our design of children's social care systems. These formed the underlying framework for what we were trying to do.

The Scale-Up project

Since 2016, we (Jenny and Rachael) have worked alongside Carlene Firmin as part of the Contextual Safeguarding programme to *do* real-life change in children's social care. In this book, we draw on our experiences as qualitative embedded researchers within multiple research projects, but substantively on our work on the national and London-based Scale-Up projects and with the London Borough of Hackney. As such, this book is the result of a shared endeavour. We are particularly grateful to Carlene Firmin, who designed many of the methods and developed and oversaw the research, as Principal Investigator. We, Rachael and Jenny, were involved in the operational management of the projects and main research elements, and we worked alongside a team of researchers, initially at the University of Bedfordshire and from 2021, at Durham University. To contextualise the methods in this book, next we give a brief overview of the research projects.

The Hackney project ran from 2018 to 2020. Jenny was an embedded researcher working with a team of social workers and youth workers employed by Hackney Council to develop an operational version of the Contextual Safeguarding framework. Jenny worked with the team from Hackney's children's social care offices two days a week. Rachael was a social work manager on this project. Once the Hackney project ended, Rachael was seconded to work for the University of Bedfordshire on the Scale-Up project, which ran from 2019 to 2022. The aim of the project was to use embedded research methods to 'scale up' the learning from the Hackney project in a group of new sites that would create bespoke versions of the Contextual Safeguarding system within their local area. Originally, a team of four researchers were employed to work in three children's social care departments (referred to as 'sites') across England and Wales. However, due to the large interest in this project, the number of sites was increased from three to five. The size of the research team increased over the lifespan of the project (from four researchers to eight) to reflect the increasing number of sites and to manage the participatory elements with young people and parents/carers. The London Scale-Up project ran from 2020 to 2022 and mirrored the national Scale-Up methodology to test and develop Contextual Safeguarding systems within four London boroughs. Rachael also worked on this project along with a research team of three.

A full methodology and outline of the Scale-Up project can be found elsewhere (Contextual Safeguarding 2022b; Firmin and Lloyd 2022), but key aspects are summarised here. The Scale-Up project ran over four years. The original intention was for a team of researchers to spend one or two days every other week in one of the five sites, meaning that each site would have a researcher physically working there approximately every three weeks. This was possible for the first year only, because from 2020, following the COVID-19 outbreak, all activity moved online until the end of the project. During the first year of the project, as you can probably imagine, travelling every other week to sites that were geographically very far from each other and far from the researchers' homes was physically and emotionally draining. But, equally, moving embedded research online was challenging in very different ways.

The project ran over four phases:

1. To begin with, the Principal Investigator established the project and started the process of recruiting sites. Research staff were hired and ethics approval applications were submitted.
2. This phase focused on understanding the current social care response to extra-familial harm. A range of methods (outlined in Part I) were used to understand and map the current children's social care response against the domains and values of the Contextual Safeguarding framework. During this phase, the project team formed relationships with sites and set up the

project. At the end of this year, the research team worked with each site to develop a plan for their new system.
3. In this phase, the research team worked with sites to actively make changes to their system, and two pilots were run in each site (Chapter 4). This involved active consultation and collaboration with sites. Due to setbacks related to COVID-19, extra time was needed for piloting and testing, so the time period for this phase was extended.
4. The final phase focused on supporting the embedding of changes into the systems and creating a toolkit of resources to help other safeguarding partners make similar changes.

In Phase 1, children's social care departments in England and Wales were invited to apply to be part of the project. Fifty areas applied for the three places available (as noted earlier, this was later increased to five). Applicants were asked to complete an expression of interest outlining the commitment from senior directors and work already undertaken to develop approaches to extra-familial harm. Shortlisted sites were invited to interview. This element of the project is important for contextualising the methods we present in this book, because it shows that, to some extent, sites had to be willing and ready to have their systems changed, including having senior buy-in. Another contextual element was that Contextual Safeguarding had relatively recently been included in statutory safeguarding guidance. This certainly increased the eagerness of sites to be involved. This was important because although we had funding to cover the research costs, sites did not receive additional funding (apart from payments made to voluntary and community sector organisations and young people taking part in the participatory research elements). But even with this perhaps unusually enabling environment, not everyone we worked with was waiting with open arms to welcome researchers in to change their system. We are confident that our commitment to taking a real-life, honest approach to the challenges encountered means that even if the circumstances of your project seem very different from the context of ours, you will find this book relatable and applicable to your situation.

Once the project was underway, the selected sites began by setting up governance arrangements. Each one formed a strategic group, made up of senior representatives from children's social care and key partner agencies (the police, education, health, youth justice and community safety), and an operational group, made up of professionals from the same agencies who were tasked with *doing* and facilitating the work and research. A single point of contact (SPOC) was identified in each site. The SPOC actively led the work and was the main contact for researchers. We also appointed a research lead to be the contact for each site SPOC. During the set-up phase, we also delivered a five-day course on Contextual Safeguarding, with each site nominating five 'champions' to participate. The course was an opportunity to learn more about the theory of Contextual Safeguarding, meet the other research sites, form relationships with the research team and gain the knowledge to roll out further training in their own sites.

Over the course of the Scale-Up project, we collected a large volume of data, including:

- 60 interviews;
- 65 focus groups;
- 68 meeting observations;
- 153 reviews of policies;
- 401 consultation activities;
- 252 case files.

These figures tell a story. They reflect a lot of work. But what is behind the numbers? The delayed trains and lost tickets, the instant (and not so instant) connections with professionals, the giggles, flip charts, coffees and sighs, the 'what should I wear?', the bad nights' sleep in unfamiliar hotels and the 'you're on mute' Teams calls. In short, the many real-life things that created these 'facts' and which we try to hold together as we tell this story.

Conclusion

We've written this book because we want to give an account of creating system change, using applied research that reflects our experiences of doing this in real life. We want to challenge the idea that doing this sort of work is straightforward and logical – like a formula for operating a machine that guarantees predictable results. While we have learnt that we need methods, tools and processes, this is not because they will somehow magically give the right answer, but because they offer helpful structure. But they are not an end in themselves. Over the course of the Scale-Up project, we learnt that the important thing is to see methods for what they are – structures for holding our anxieties, our conversations, our need to improve services, all of which are complex and messy. If we think of system change as a tree, the methods presented in Part I are the trunk and branches. The explorations of relationships, emotion and culture in Part II are the roots, providing the connections underground to sustain what's above. In Part III, we first look up at the fruit – the actual system changes made – and then down at the ground – the conceptual underpinning that keeps the whole thing steady. We hope this holistic picture makes you feel excited about this interconnected approach to systems change research. We want you to see its possibilities and experience its rewards. As you set out, we hope you find this book to be a practical, thought-provoking and inspirational companion.

PART I

Methods for understanding and changing children's social care systems

This is a poem about our joint experiences of doing embedded research. It draws on the embodied, emotional and relational processes that we experienced when we entered this role. To write this combined poem we re-entered moments in time by repeating the word 'it's' – that is, it's like this, it's like that … etc., trying to draw on the immediacy of the things that happened. This helped us to re-enter the field through our imagination and write Part II in a way that was in touch with these experiences. If you want to explore an experience in a creative and unconventional way, try using the same provocation 'It's' to write your own reflective poem.

It's should I use this chair?

It's do I have my pass?
                      Does it work?
It's awkwardly tailgating up the stairs
                      Till I'm stuck
It's smiling through the glass
                      Does anyone know me?
It's 'We didn't realise you were here today!'
                      Four hours 36 minutes, one
bus, two tubes, two trains to get here …

Its 'I'll show you the kitchen   just don't use <u>this</u> fridge'

It's should I use this chair? Can I lower it? Will that be annoying? I don't want to be annoying.
It's the smart wheely case in the corner

                        Self-consciously cosmopolitan
                        and southern
                        Can I leave my stuff here?

It's sitting in the corner of the office
'Does the Wi-Fi work for you love?'
It's slightly panicked professionals rushing round

'There must be something for her to do'
It's being amenable
                        Smiling and smiling, don't
                        worry about it
                        It's when's my train home?

It's boredom and stress: three hours 18 minutes till
I leave
It's no outdoor light in this office
Its feeling left out
                        Overhearing snippets of
                        conversations
                        A worried worker asks
'Has mum been away <u>all night</u>?'

It's seeing a practitioner you know – hello, hello!
            'How you doing, Jen?'
                        It's shortening my name
     Jenny   Jen
                        It's forgetting <u>her</u> name

Is now a good time to go out for lunch?
Will I be able to get back in?
It's feeling very tired
It's what's the point of me being here?
It's what do <u>they</u> think I'm here for?

Then suddenly
It's 'Can you speak to this social worker?'
                        Of course, of course, I want to
                        be useful

Part I

                But does my accent stand out?
Do I sound very English?
            It's what do I say to this social worker about a child who has been shot?
                Its 'OK thank you   that's helpful'
                Was it?
                I don't think it was

It's where's my ticket?
It's thank you for having me
It's making sure I wash up my cup
It's sitting on the train   writing up my notes

2

Embedded methods for learning how the system works

Introduction

Part I of this book is about the methods, or tools, we use for understanding and changing children's social care systems. But we want to be clear: there is no such thing as a perfect tool or way to collect information. We can never know everything about a system and how it works. It is important that you know this before you read this part of the book. We don't want you to be under the illusion that this chapter and the next two are going to offer *the* way to understanding complex systems. All systems are complex, but children's social care by its very nature is subjective and relational, messy and ever-changing. If you are setting out on a voyage to change a social care system, it will help you to know now that it won't be smooth sailing. Despite your beautiful spreadsheet and colour-coded timetable, your plans will be immediately disrupted by the relational aspects of this work: a central person will leave; a new director will change everything at the last minute; you won't get on with everyone. These relational aspects of system change are discussed in Part II, but they are integral to our way of working, so you would do well to hold them in mind as you move through the chapters in Part I.

If even the best-laid plans are derailed, if it's such a messy business, why do we need a research plan, structure and methods at all? It might sound contradictory, but we have found that using a consistent set of tools is nonetheless central to the work of creating system change in children's services. Not because they give you an objective way to map and record systems, but because the feeling of being tasked with changing children's social care systems is daunting and overwhelming. The tools you use are important because when you turn up to work you need something – anything – to help you make sense of the complexity, confusion and mess. You will regularly ask yourself 'what am I meant to be doing?' and question if you're doing it right. Having a structure helps to calm that part of our anxious minds so that we can move on with our task. The important thing is not to cling too much to the structure but to remember that no matter which tool or method you use, the point is not to get it 'right' but to learn about the system in a consistent, thoughtful and sensitive way. Our tools helped us to piece together each small bit of information into the larger whole and understand how they fitted together, and we hope they will support you to do this too.

To capture the differences between our tools for changing systems, we have categorised them into three groups: ethnographic methods; discursive methods; and reciprocal methods. Ethnographic methods are activities that helped us form a holistic picture of how the system operated in practice. These included meeting observations and workplace ethnography, covered in this chapter. The discursive methods we used included reviewing written documents, such as case files, assessments, plans and policy documents, and these are covered in Chapter 3. The reciprocal methods we used involved us, the researchers, contributing more directly to supporting the practitioners we were working with, either through consultatory activities or activities like training, and these are described in Chapter 4. Other methods, such as focus groups and interviews, were used throughout the project but mostly towards the latter stages of our involvement when we were seeking to understand new ways of working that were being piloted. We do not provide a detailed account of these methods in this book as they are well covered elsewhere.

If you are coming to this book as a social researcher, you may feel more comfortable with ethnographic methods, like observation. You may feel struck with fear at the thought of reciprocal methods that require you to give advice, 'do favours' and share your opinion in the moment. There can be nothing scarier than having a practitioner turn to you at the end of a meeting observation and asking 'so what do you think we should do?' Or you might be someone who feels comfortable with reciprocal activities and more daunted by the 'traditional' academic methods. Either way, try to adopt an open attitude to both approaches and learn as you go. This is the best way to allow these tools to support you to build a picture of what is happening in the system, rather than getting hung up on whether you're doing it 'right'.

We want this book to be useful, so instead of giving a comprehensive list and going into the theoretical and ethical ins and outs of each method, we offer lively examples of the main methods we used alongside exercises to help you think about how you could use them too. Whether you already know the system you're setting out to change or it is brand new to you, we strongly recommend that you follow a systematic and rigorous process for finding out what is going on and in a way that draws on multiple perspectives and a variety of sources. For us, this meant starting with methods that were about looking and listening to what was going on. Our approach centred on spending time with and in the systems we were helping to change, being as 'embedded' as possible in the children's social care systems that we were working with. We sat alongside teams, observing their day-to-day work, discussing what was going on, gradually building partnerships and learning as much as we could before we started suggesting changes.

You could think of this chapter as your guide to the early stage of system change. You are sitting on the riverbank, looking over the edge at the water flowing below. As we guide you through our methods, think of them as floats to help you overcome your nerves and get ready for the water. This chapter is about learning without disturbing the flow and using the water's reflection to really see what is going on in the whole environment. Gradually, as relationships and our knowledge developed, we needed different methods that allowed us to get involved in the systems we were changing, to dip our toes in and even take the plunge, and this is the focus of Chapters 3 and 4. But for now, it's about taking it all in. So open your eyes and let's begin.

Mapping the social care system

At the start of Scale-Up, we wanted to understand how each site responded to extra-familial harm – what helped and what hindered. As we were trying to change an aspect of children's social care, it is helpful to set out an overview of the English child protection system (you may be looking at a different area but the same idea applies). Figure 2.1. provides a visual image of this, annotated with the methods we used at each stage, which we will come back to.

In England, if people are worried that a child is a risk of significant harm, they can make a referral to children's social care. In this case, the 'people' are usually educators, health workers or the police, but they could be anyone. 'Significant harm' is the wording used in the English law that underpins how the child safeguarding system operates (the Children Act 1989).

Let's say an Accident and Emergency doctor sees a child with a stab wound. Hopefully, they would make a safeguarding referral to a children's social care department. This referral (which could be a written form or a telephone call) would go to a 'front door service' where a person (usually a social worker) would review the information (called screening) and decide if this child has reached a threshold for a response by children's social care. If the child wasn't already 'open' to children's social care (for example, they don't already have a social worker working with them and it's the first time social care have heard about this child), they would (hopefully) refer this child for an assessment. We say 'hopefully' because even though being the victim of a stab wound is usually significantly harmful, the child might not always be referred on for a statutory assessment. This is one the many challenges of the current response to extra-familial harm that we documented in our research (Lloyd and Firmin 2020).

But let's imagine that a referral is made, and a practitioner is tasked with doing an assessment of that child and their family. The assessment requires them to consider three things: the 'child's developmental needs'; 'parenting capacity'; and 'family environment factors' (these are laid out in statutory guidance, *Working Together to Safeguard Children*; HM Government 2018). The assessment process can involve multiple things, such as reviewing records held by health services and contacting the school or other partners, including the police. It would likely also involve visiting the child and their parents or carers. The practitioner doing the assessment will keep a note of all of this in case notes held on a safeguarding computer system. As part of this process, and depending in which local authority this child lives, there may be several different meetings focused on understanding and reducing the risk posed to this child. Let's say that during the assessment, the social worker starts to suspect the child is being exploited to sell drugs. It is likely other meetings would be held where the practitioner doing the assessment could talk about their concerns. These meetings may be 'multi-agency', with different safeguarding partners – perhaps education, health, police and community safety – coming together.

Finally, the practitioner would hold a planning meeting where different partners would work together and the family and child may be invited to join in to contribute to a plan. The plan would focus on how to respond to the harm and hopefully minimise risk and increase safety. Throughout this process, social workers would decide on the level of harm the child is experiencing, and these would correspond with what the law and policy say this child can expect. The practitioner may then continue to work with the family and child, following the plan and meeting regularly, with the ultimate aim of keeping the child safe (and ensuring the 'case can be closed').

Figure 2.1 has two purposes. First, it shows a simplified picture of the children's social care system. You might find it helpful at the start of your system change work to think about a hypothetical person/situation that relates to your research aim and ask: How might this person/situation interact with each element of the system? How would they 'move' through the system? What would determine the responses they get at each stage? Exercise 2.1 can guide you through this. Second, Figure 2.1 is a gateway into the methods and tools described in Part I. It gives an overview of the different ways you can learn about the system. The annotations along the sides are activities relevant to specific parts of the system, and in the centre are more generic methods that can be used throughout. You may want to refer back to Figure 2.1 to anchor yourself and review your options for which method or tool to use next.

Figure 2.1: The child and family social care system, annotated with methods

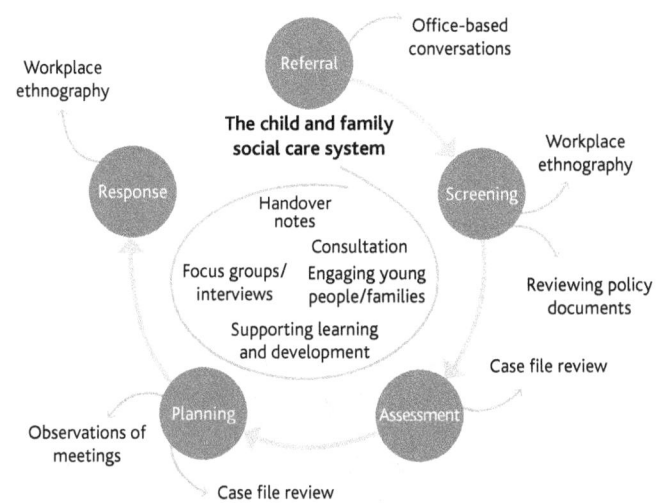

Exercise 2.1: Mapping

- Think about the system you are trying to change. Take a piece of paper and follow these steps:
  1. Start by mapping out how you think it works (maybe you don't know yet).
  2. Think about where key decisions are made in the system.
  3. If you don't know, map some of the first ways you could find out (you might list the people you need to speak to or the research to read).
- Start to note ideas about methods you could use to understand the different aspects of the system.

Choosing your methods

We outlined in Chapter 1 the importance of having a research aim. Our aim was to understand more about how to create children's social care systems that address extra-familial harm to children and young people. Developing and adapting the Contextual

Safeguarding framework was the way we sought to do this. We followed a three-stage process: understanding the system; piloting approaches; and embedding change. As you might expect, the first stage was all about finding out what was going on, but looking back we can see that this process served other purposes too, ones that were not so obvious to us at the start (we didn't have a book like this to read!). In retrospect, we can see that the three main functions of this stage and the tools we used were to:

- understand how the current safeguarding system addresses extra-familial harm to children and young people, and the enablers and barriers of this;
- form relationships with people in the research sites (this is covered more in Part II);
- represent and hold the research and practice relationship sufficiently to have credibility to create system changes (covered in Part II).

Knowing what it is you are trying to understand and what sources of information are available to you is crucial to identifying which methods you need to use. If the system you are working in doesn't use case notes, for example, this won't be part of your research design. But while what you choose to look at and how you do it is important, it's also important to remember that methods are more than just learning about the system. As we explore in Part II, methods are also vital to help us form relationships which are central to system change. For this reason, as you set out, we encourage you to keep an open mind about the particular tools you use and not get too hung up on whether they're the 'right' ones. We suggest that you start out, as we did, with tools that allow you to gently begin to observe, learn and listen, ask questions and get to know people, which in research terms we call ethnographic methods.

> **Exercise 2.2: Aims**
>
> 1. Start by thinking about what the aim of your research/ project is. Write a sentence to capture it.

2. What are the gaps in your understanding about the system you are researching?

3. How can being embedded in the system you want to change help you? It helped us in three ways, but you might have more.

Ethnographic methods

Ethnography is a research term to describe a type of qualitative research that focuses on understanding the environment and culture of a group of people by spending time with them and getting to know how they live/work (O'Reilly 2012). When we use this approach to understand professional life, we spend time in the organisation in question, usually over several months or even longer, and use a range of research tools to build a detailed picture of what is going on. In the children's social care systems that we worked in, we drew on the ethnographic tools of observing meetings, workplace ethnography, focus groups and interviews to do this. Here we focus on the first two.

Meeting observations

> ### VIGNETTE OF A MEETING OBSERVATION
>
> Picture the scene: You arrive at a meeting room; a couple of people are inside; you enter but you don't recognise anyone there (or perhaps you enter the online 'room'). You check you're in the right place, and someone invites you to take a seat and asks you where you're from. You explain who you are and that you are there to observe the meeting. You remind them of the email you sent with the information sheet and check they are happy for you to take notes. They say they are, but you don't seem convinced they understand what you're doing. As more people enter, you start to worry there might not be enough seats and if you're taking up someone else's space. You worry about the fact that the new people didn't hear you explain who you are. Have they consented to being part of the research? Should you pipe up again? But this would disrupt the flow of the meeting. You awkwardly move to a seat in the corner, away from the table. After a few minutes of polite small talk, the meeting starts and everyone introduces themselves. You are halfway through writing the acronym of someone's job title and trying to understand who they work for when the next person starts talking and you miss the name of their organisation. The meeting continues very fast. Someone states that since the last meeting they have updated the TOR of the MAPPA meeting and that the MACE meeting needs to be updated to meet the strategic priorities listed under two – point – four – point – three. Then they move to a discussion of 'cases' and start talking about the first young person, called Tom. He moved from 'a four' to 'a seven' due to going missing, and a strategy meeting was held. You try and write down everything as quickly as you can, but you lose track as you try and figure out if the woman called Aisha is from the police or youth justice and wonder what 'a four' or 'a seven' means. You can tell that Martin seems a bit annoyed at Claire, but you're

Embedded methods

not sure why, so you just carry on writing. Then you realise halfway through what MET stands for and you try to change your notes. Someone makes a joke, and everyone laughs and you feel a bit relieved because it gives you time to catch up. Welcome to the ethnographic tool of meeting observations!

This vignette paints a realistic picture of how confusing it can be to observe a meeting, especially when the terminology is unfamiliar to you. But don't be put off by this – it can be a very useful tool for building a picture of the system. In its simplest form, meeting observations can help you capture data about the discussions and actions that take place in a meeting. Alongside factual information about what happens, you are also trying to work out how what you see in this meeting fits with the rest of the system. When we observed meetings, we wanted to understand how professionals made decisions about children or contexts that were associated with extra-familial harm. Observing meetings helped us to understand two crucial elements of the children's social care teams that we worked in – the *system processes* and the *culture* that underpinned the decisions that were made. By attending meetings, we built a picture of who made decisions and on what basis they made them, and over time we gained a sense of the cultural influences on how these decisions were made. For example, we observed the power dynamics underpinning these processes. We asked ourselves questions like: Who talks most? Who is present and who is absent? How are decisions made? What is the tone of what is being said? These helped us to contextualise the overarching purpose of every meeting observation, which was to give an accurate account of what happened.

Which meetings?

The first task is to identify which meetings you want to observe. You might be tempted to observe every meeting possible due to fear that you might miss *the* important meeting and because having 'something' in your diary can help mitigate the feeling that you're not doing enough. As that would not be feasible, it is important to think about which meetings you should be observing. Return to Exercises 2.1 and 2.2 to help you plan which meetings to attend. As our focus was on extra-familial harm, we asked to be invited to any meetings where children experiencing extra-familial harm would be discussed or any meetings where locations where children encountered harm would be discussed. This meant we were invited to the following types of meeting:

- multi-agency child exploitation meetings, where children experiencing, or at risk of experiencing, sexual or criminal exploitation were discussed;
- policing, youth justice or community safety meetings, where children experiencing extra-familial harm may have been discussed and social work were present;
- individual case discussions, such as child protection conferences or strategy meetings for individual children;
- team meetings, such as front door meetings, where decisions about threshold were made.

Although each of the children's social care systems we worked in had a different arrangement in terms of meetings, they were similar in that they held so many of them! In general, it is good to check with your site contact to make sure that you are not missing a meeting or being asked to attend a meeting that has little relevance for your work.

What do I do?

Meeting observations can be quite daunting at first because you are required to be physically present and, as the story at the start of the section on meeting observations showed, much of what happens is out of your control. Essentially though, in observing a meeting, it is your job to collect data on what happens that can be analysed at a later point. To support us with this task, we used 'observation templates'. These have advantages and disadvantages. Some disadvantages are that there can be a temptation to have too many sections in the template – so many that you spend most of the meeting trying to figure out what is meant to go where. A colleague of ours remarked that while working on one project (where she was junior to other researchers) she felt so worried about whether she was completing the template in 'the right way' that she felt unable to really understand what was happening in the meeting. And if you're using your computer to fill in a template, formatting and word processing software is not always your friend, and this can be quite stressful when trying to document everything. Despite this, there are advantages of observation templates – mainly that they give you *something* to do. Having a template makes you feel you have a task, and if you can't do anything else, you can at least write down what is being said. They also allow consistency in how notes are recorded and ensure that crucial information (the date, for example) isn't missed. There may be times when it is not appropriate for you to write notes during the meeting. It is important that you use your discretion and be sensitive to those involved. For example, we decided not to take notes during a child protection conference meeting when we were sitting next to a family member, out of sensitivity to them and not wanting to cause a distraction.

> **Exercise 2.3: Making an observation template**
>
> If you don't have a clear idea of what you want to focus on, a basic template might include:
>
> - some notes at the top to remind you/others what to do – for example, the aim of the observation and your commitment to ethics (like making sure the people involved know why you are there and checking they have agreed that you can observe them);
> - who/which organisations are present (and who is missing);
> - what happens or what is said;
> - what you think is happening 'beneath the surface' – for example, how the meeting makes you think or feel (you could add these notes in brackets or in a separate column);
> - what actions or decisions are made;
> - a section for reflections afterwards.
>
> You can find an example of an observation template in our online toolkit.

Observation strategies

Our largest research project involved eight researchers working across nine children's services – all were observing meetings and recording notes. To manage this, we needed some consistency and a shared set of aims. However, it was also important for each researcher to draw on their different strengths when observing meetings. Inevitably, this resulted in variation in the way researchers took to the task of meeting observations. Within our team, we developed three broad approaches to documenting observations: 'say what you see'; 'say what you think'; 'say what you feel'.

If you are new to observing meetings or you are managing a team of researchers, 'say what you see' might be the easiest approach to take. This involves writing down as much information as possible (which can be quite hard). You write down what is said and what happens and don't worry too much about what it means. At the start of the project, this was our main approach when writing observation notes, and it helped us to become familiar with the sites and the task at hand. We suggest you start with this approach, prioritising writing down the facts about the meetings you observe, leaving the analysis for later. The following is an example of 'say what you see' taken from our own observation notes for a multi-agency child exploitation meeting where professionals were discussing a list of children and their concerns about their safety:

EXTRACT FROM
MEETING OBSERVATION TEMPLATE

YP [young person] 5 – 15 years. Possession of cannibals, feels unsafe in his area, wants to be placed out of area. Wants to be placed on his own not with other children. He says he is kicking off because he wants to be on his own. Not saying why he feels unsafe. Recently moved, but his placement has given notice so he is moving to another placement – the staff cannot manage him. He is placed out of area and he wouldn't be brought back. Stealing, arrested in relation to damage to property, indecent images on his phone – staff took it off him. Chair: 'Do we think he is being exploited or doing it on his own free will?' No concerns of organised crime – he is 'just causing havoc'. Concerns about a conversation with the older brother about killing someone.

In this extract, the researcher documents what is said with minimal comment. Direct quotes are shown through use of quotation marks, where possible noting who was speaking. The description is written clearly so that someone who wasn't there can get a sense of what happened and make their own analysis. Of course, these notes are not completely 'objective' (nor do they strive to be); what the researcher decides to quote is likely to be influenced by their own analysis and feelings about what is said. In this case, perhaps they considered 'just causing havoc' to be particularly noteworthy.

Similar to 'say what you see', 'say what you think' involves writing a description of what is happening, but the observer also notes any thoughts they have in response to what they observe. Writing notes in this way allows the observer to draw on these initial thoughts later when they come to analysing the observation notes. An example of this approach is shown in the next extract, which is from a meeting observation that took place as part of a location assessment – the researcher writes their thoughts and reflections using bullets and italics:

EXTRACT FROM MEETING OBSERVATION TEMPLATE

When disruption of adults takes place, kids become more vulnerable. Need to make sure safeguarding is in place. If something significant changes within the group then get in touch with [team name] immediately.

- *Would be interesting to know what is being put in place for this?*

Idea is to protect the children, may see increase in potential arrest, idea is to disrupt what is going on.

- *Bit of a concern here as to what the purpose of this exercise is – is the aim to arrest the adults at all costs? Can this possibly be welfare led if it leads to YP [young people] being arrested?*

Doesn't need to be mentioned in CP [child protection] meetings, etc., only say 'part of assessments'.

- *The way the police are so central to this process means its not possible to integrate it with CP processes – practitioners cannot even talk about the young people involved. Implication that this is very police centred.*

The third option, 'say what you feel', incorporates both of the previous approaches but also adds descriptions that dynamically draw on the observer's feelings, interpretations and analysis of what might be going on in the meeting. 'Feelings' here might be an overriding emotion (such as sadness) that the observer feels is dominating the discussion but not necessarily explicitly expressed, but it could also mean describing subtle things that they notice about interactions or things that are absent. This is about reflecting on what might be 'beneath the surface' of the meeting – at the level of dynamics, emotions and relationships. In the next example, where the researcher is in a child protection conference, we have underlined the researcher reflections, based on their perception of what might be happening underneath the surface:

EXTRACT FROM MEETING OBSERVATION TEMPLATE

School reported that she was excluded from school for fighting with a pupil. It was mentioned, almost as an aside, that it was probably linked to her being teased about her mother being a drug taker. This was not interrogated by the conference. School also reports that she is on a different timetable to mainstream, but she wants to be on mainstream. No one asked why she was not keeping to her alternative timetable or why she is not turning up to school on time (she is often late). After the conference, once school rep had left, there was a feeling by those still in the room that school had been 'harsh'.

They felt that they had not considered how not being with her friends on the same timetable was important to the YP [young person]. Someone said, 'it's no wonder she wasn't coming back to lessons, because it means leaving her friends'. It was also clearly

> the case that social workers did not feel able to challenge the school about what they felt were harsh and punitive measures (exclusion, restricted timetable), which were in response to the YP being unable to regulate her feelings at school. Someone said she thought the school had all had attachment training.

This extract helps to put you right in the room and gives space to the feelings and general mood of how the meeting was conducted. To write in this way, you need to be sensitive to things like body language and tone of voice, which, with a bit of practice, most people can do. What is perhaps harder is seeing this way of writing as 'rigorous' research. In this book, we argue for doing just that – tuning in to the complexity and dynamism of human interactions and taking this seriously. If we want our system change to be close to 'real life', then tuning in to the messy, complex and relational dynamics will support us to do this. These things are not a distraction but, as we explore in Part II, a vital way in to understanding and working with the system as it really is.

But it is not easy. It can be hard to add these types of comments without losing track of what is being said, so we suggest you 'say what you see' in the moment and soon after add your thoughts and feelings, making clear the difference between what was observed and what is reflection or analysis. This can be time-consuming and laborious, so make sure to account for this when you plan observations. Writing and adding to notes can take as long as the meeting itself!

For all three ways of writing observation notes, we advise adding a 'post-meeting reflection' section to your observation template. The following shows what this might include:

MEETING REFLECTION
Like in the past conference, the carer was not the source of the 'blame' for the harm. However the responsibility (and therefore, implicitly the blame) was very much with the young person. The plan was completely dependent upon his personal motivation to change and therefore seemed to me to be quite fragile, particularly when his personal/internal sense of self, his feelings and ability to regulate were not explored and the

plan contained very little attention to digging into this as a way of understanding his drug taking or anger. There was likewise no curiosity or sense that the professional might look to the social aspect of his drug taking as the focus for reducing his likelihood of taking.

Undertaking observations can be daunting for multiple reasons, but a strategy that encompasses writing down what you see, think and feel is a good option for anyone starting out with this tool. Observing meetings helped us to understand how decisions were made, what the process was and where this sat within the system. But they also allowed us to understand the 'culture' of how the system operates – for example, the tensions between organisations, how professionals spoke about children and how they challenged one another.

Ethics of observation

With all ethnographic methods, ethics and consent can be complicated (Ferguson 2014; McGinity and Salokangas 2014; Lloyd 2021), so it's important to be reflexive and flexible. During the initial set-up of our project, we asked for consent from heads of service to attend meetings where no young people or families were present. But we also made sure that ahead of each meeting, we sent information sheets to everyone invited to the meeting, giving them the option to say that they did not want to be part of an observation. At that point, if someone said they did not want to be part of the research, we did not attend. For the meetings we did attend, we anonymised our observation notes at the point of writing them so that names and locations were protected straight away. If we wanted to observe a meeting where a young person or parent/carer was present, then the consent process depended on the situation and generally involved asking for consent ahead of time via the practitioner who was leading the meeting and then checking again on the day to see whether they were still happy for us to be there. In every meeting, we introduced ourselves and explained why we were there. We never recorded audio of meetings. Although this would have been really useful data, we felt it was safer and less daunting for the people being observed if we wrote notes instead, and, as mentioned, sometimes even this was done after rather than during a meeting if that seemed most appropriate.

Workplace ethnography

Choosing the right combination of research methods to reach your aim – a process known in research terms as developing a methodology – is like building a house. Things like mapping out the system, observing meetings and running focus groups are like the bricks, creating support and structure for how you will spend your time. This is important because you will need activities to be getting on with, whether you are physically present within the system you are involved in changing, mostly online or a hybrid of the two. But a house of just bricks will fall down without cement to hold it together. We turn now to those practices which sat alongside the more formal methods we used, which held things together. For us, the cement was found in the informal, less traditional opportunities that opened up through being embedded in children's social care teams.

We do not wish to romanticise these methods. Many of our projects required working with a great deal of uncertainty, which was often challenging. In the Scale-Up project, for example, we travelled large distances to spend one or two days in a site every few weeks. While we tried to book things like meeting observations in advance, we often had to just 'go with the flow' of what was happening on the day. Because we were not sitting with teams every day, we relied on the SPOC to organise our days, but they did not always have the time to arrange full days for us. Often, planning our time sat on top of their already very busy schedule and, as we explore more in Part II, we sometimes felt awkward about this extra burden and looked for ways to compensate. On more than one occasion, we travelled over five hours to arrive at the site only to be greeted by a surprised professional saying they 'didn't realise you were coming today'. Often the rest of the day would be spent sitting with slightly bemused practitioners as people scurried around trying to find things for us to do. It is perhaps because of this uncertainty that we created and often clung to templates and tables as a way to find some meaning and structure to our task. These things helped us handle how scary it felt to turn up to a new place as an outsider with the task of getting to know their children's social care system. But, despite how unsettling a lack of structure could be, if we were flexible and adapted to the situation, many opportunities arose for learning. We describe two of these opportunities next.

Opportunistic office-based conversations

When we started our project, we hoped to be able to sit with teams to understand how they worked and fitted in with the rest of the system, but this often didn't play out. In reality, our days varied significantly – one day we might be given a personal tour guide who explained everything and let us join them for all their meetings, but another day we'd be sat in the corner alone with nobody knowing what to do with us! However, one way or another we did spend time in the following service areas/teams: the front door service; assessment teams; adolescent services; exploitation teams; youth justice teams; and practice development teams.

We learnt to make the most of the unpredictability of our days by looking for opportunities to engage the people around us in conversations about their work. We began by assuming that the practitioner had little or no idea about the project we were working on, so we would describe why we were there and then lead into asking about how this related to them. Here's an example of the sort of descriptions we gave:

> ### INTRODUCING THE RESEARCH
> The project we are working on is trying to create better systems that respond to children that get harmed outside of their home. This might be children that experience child sexual exploitation or violence. The child protection system is set up to focus on parents and doesn't always know how to work with children experiencing harm with their peers. Do you come into contact with children experiencing this harm? How does it work in your team? Have you noticed any problems?

Sometimes, if we were hoping to learn a lot about the way the service was structured, we felt frustrated at having 'only' had conversations with the people sat around us. In hindsight, however, we can see that these conversations gave us information about the culture of systems that we then used to contextualise other observations. How available and friendly practitioners were to us, for example, could tell us a lot about what it was like to work there. The following extracts are from 'handover notes' (discussed in the next subsection) after a day spent in two services in the same area:

> HANDOVER NOTES
> I went and sat with the [service] in [region] for the day. All in all it wasn't so helpful because there wasn't much on. But it was helpful to visit the [building], which is one of their [services] in [location]. This [building] has the [service names] (although I didn't meet them).
>
> Off the record: [location] is held up to be a not good area in terms of practice. Historically a service manager took over and as a result lots of social workers left. There has been a high turnover of staff. They now have a new manager from [location] who is trying to fix it. They have been in position for a few weeks. This might explain why we haven't spent any time there.

As the extracts show, the benefit of sitting with teams is that it allows practitioners to get to know you enough to share things that are 'off the record'. While we would not use this in any formal way, it helped us to understand some of the historic issues in that place, which was helpful when we came to supporting changes to their system. Sitting with people and having informal conversations opened unexpected avenues for learning about the systems and building trusting relationships. The last two extracts are also an example of the final research tool described in this chapter – handover notes.

Handover notes

The initial Scale-Up project team involved three researchers who lived far apart from each other, each travelling to one of five sites approximately every fortnight. If we weren't on a long train ride to one site, we were planning a trip to another. We had regular reflective meetings as a team, but we needed a process to help us hold our thoughts and feelings in the times between these and our visits. The process we used involved handover notes – a live word document in which we recorded the types of things we might have otherwise talked about had we shared an office together. Each site had its own handover notes document, which would be updated after each visit. We would write a summary of the visit and anything not recorded via another process (like a meeting observation template), including project updates, system changes, reflections on the site culture or the different relationships we formed. The handover notes helped us to build on each other's work in a consistent way as we travelled between sites. Over time, they also formed a holistic qualitative picture of the systemic, relational and cultural changes that happened in each site, as we experienced them.

We share two extracts from handover notes here. Although they contain potentially confusing acronyms and specific details, we have kept those in to give a feel for the types of information we documented:

HANDOVER NOTES
Discussion around anxieties held [by practitioners] regarding pilot one and integrating Contextual Safeguarding into existing child protection processes rather than creating new pathways. [Researcher] alleviated some anxieties by giving an overview of what other research sites are doing and our confidence in the process undertaken to gain consensus among professionals – e.g. via in-depth discussion at Task and Finish Group.

In this example, we hear about the worries that practitioners shared with a researcher about a pilot study taking place as part of the project. This could help the researcher who was next visiting this site to be aware of these anxious feelings and give her some ideas for how to manage these, particularly if she is less experienced in embedded research. In-person (rather than online) visits often involved practitioners sharing their worries with us about the system changes we were seeking to make together. We also found that professionals were happier sharing these with us in informal settings than they were in the more formal meetings that involved the research leader and managers. This meant that handover notes were important for reflecting some of the more hidden shifts going on through the process of system change.

The next extract reflects the unexpected and unpredictable nature of embedded work and the importance of handover notes for capturing these more lively moments of learning:

> #### HANDOVER NOTES
> While I was there in the site there was a developing issue. A young person had gone missing. There were concerns he may have been kidnapped following a stabbing and a group had turned up at his house. A primary challenge appeared to be that social workers were not able to assess the risk level posed to the young person. I joined a meeting over the phone with police who were stating that it was not high risk based on their investigation but that they couldn't share what the intelligence was that this was based on.

This example shows how being present in a site and sitting with a team can provide rich opportunities for learning about what's going on. Re-reading this note, I (Jenny) am taken back to the moment it occurred. I can vividly remember the office, the phone call with the police officers and the discussion between practitioners in the room. I can remember the shock I felt on hearing the mention of kidnappers wearing balaclavas and the effort it took to stifle my complete horror at what they were saying. But the note also reminds me of how, despite a child potentially having been kidnapped, people seemed to be preoccupied with technical talk about 'risk levels' and procedures. After the meeting, social workers talked to me about how hard it was for them to get the information they needed from the police to help them understand the danger posed to children. This example shows that handover notes were not only very important during the process of the research, but also helped us, retrospectively, to quickly access and review our learning as we have gone back to analyse and make sense of things. Even if you are the only researcher or local system change leader, we recommend that you keep a similar record of your informal thoughts, feelings and observations to support you to value, hold and analyse important information about the structural, relational and cultural aspects of system change.

Conclusion

Researching and leading change in children's social care systems takes courage. We need to adopt a fairly intrepid attitude as we face the unknown system and the unknown relationships and emotions that are contained within it. We need to uphold a sense of hope that change is possible but at the same time stay grounded and realistic about the limits of how far we can control this. The system we end up with will always look different from the one we thought we were creating, and there will certainly be obstacles along the way. But we have written this book because we can attest to the reality that doing system change in children's social care is a richly rewarding and valuable thing to engage in. For us, the thing that helped us keep going in the midst of uncertainty was having a grounded structure and set of tools to trust in. We didn't exactly know at the time how well our tools would 'work', but although (as we are at pains to underline) they are not an end in themselves, they were vital for anchoring the process. This chapter has explored methods that can help us get started. In Chapter 3, to continue the river analogy, we move closer to and start to get into the water. We close the chapter with some key pointers:

1. Keep a sticky note to remind yourself that there is no perfect tool or research design – if it didn't feel messy, confusing and overwhelming, then it wouldn't be work that resembled real life.
2. Work slowly and systematically to map and understand your system – take your time and draw in other people and perspectives.
3. Get your aim clear in your mind before you start, and then choose your methods with that in mind, and not the other way around.

4. Make templates to hold information, but don't get too hung up on them. Try to record what you see during observations, and later add what you think and feel.
5. Be as flexible as you can and try to embrace the uncertainty – some of our most valuable learning came through unplanned, opportunistic moments.
6. Keep a record of your thoughts and reflections. Value this as much as you do recording information about meetings structures and processes.

3

Methods for actively engaging with the system

Introduction

VIGNETTE SHOWING THE MESSY NATURE OF ENGAGEMENT

During the Scale-Up project, a relatively new research assistant was asked to observe an online meeting held within a research site. Usually, more senior researchers would accompany research assistants, but as no one was available and it was online, the team felt they would be ok alone this time. This meeting was one of many to discuss the site's pilot, which would involve testing a new statutory child protection pathway for children harmed outside the home. Although there were numerous technical questions related to the law, policy and ethics of such an approach to be ironed out, this shouldn't have mattered too much, because the research assistant only needed to observe and (as we discussed in Chapter 2) write what she saw, thought and felt. Unfortunately, halfway through the meeting the new senior director, hearing that someone from the Contextual Safeguarding research team was in the meeting, addressed her directly and asked: 'So, what is the position of the university on whether cases should be held at child in need or child protection?' Despite feeling very put on the spot, the research assistant gave the perfectly appropriate answer – that this was something the pilot was hoping to understand. The senior director replied, curtly, that these cases were very high risk and that it was 'them' and not 'us' who had to hold that risk. After the meeting, the research assistant joined a call with the team. She was upset and cried as she talked about how it had felt. Later she reflected on how it had felt like she was being called out as an imposter by the most senior person in the room.

We would like to be able to say that we are sharing this story as a cautionary tale so that you can minimise the risk of these instances happening in your work. Certainly, there are things we could have done differently, like clarifying our role to the site, better prepping the research assistant or having a rule that they shouldn't be expected to observe meetings alone. But, in reality, no matter how much we tried to develop shared expectations with our site partners, these types of messy misalignments were a regular feature of the work. Embedded research, along with action research and participatory methods, are founded on the principle of collaboration between researchers and people who live and work in the systems being changed (McGinity and Salokangas 2014). There is often an assumption that at the very least those working in collaboration have agreed how they want to work together – the terms of engagement. But, in our experience, this is rarely the case. For us, the way you interact with sites has to be flexible and iterative – which are perhaps fancy words for saying that, to a large extent, we need to muddle through, be open to being surprised and try to keep up. To go back to our river analogy, no matter how much you try to put neat boundaries around things, hoping to stay dry on the riverbank, however much you cling to your tools like buoys to keep you afloat, at any moment you might be pulled into the rapids and off you go!

In this chapter, we are delving into the relational methods we used to understand systems. Relationships are dynamic and active, so in this chapter we're looking at methods that involve actively engaging with the system. But these are not relationships for their own sake; drawing on action research principles, they were relationships formed for the purpose of creating change (Koshy 2005). Our aim was to form partnerships with people in sites where we actively shared in the change process (Meyer 2000). Although

Chapter 2 describes ethnographic methods that involve watching and learning, the reality is that passive observation is never really an option within embedded research. So, let's look at those tools that support us to be *active* in learning about and changing systems, starting with 'discursive methods', and then moving to the most active of our relational tools, 'reciprocal methods'. It's time to get into the water and start making ripples and waves.

Discursive methods

Perhaps it sounds counterintuitive to describe methods that allow us to be active as 'discursive'. When you think of being active, focusing on discourse and language construction within systems (Yardley 2013) may not be the first thing that comes to mind. But in fact we found that examining the language in written texts produced by sites gave us a foundation to do active system change work, because the focus was on the texts rather than our impressions. Many of the methods we employed involved elements of discursive analysis. For example, we reviewed policy documents by either commenting on how existing policies could be more aligned with Contextual Safeguarding or by noting draft policy revisions. Here, we focus in on the discursive method that we found most instrumental for facilitating change: case file review.

Case file review

Case file review involves looking at a set of individual social care records using a pre-agreed set of parameters. The intention is to understand something about what happened when those 'cases' came into contact with the local social care system. We want to know things like: What services did they receive? How were they written about? How were decisions made about them? When did the case close? We follow the convention of using the word 'cases', but already this confronts us with how challenging this method can be, because of course we are really talking about children, not 'cases' – a term which creates distance by prioritising procedural language.

Our focus in case review was the database records of children who had been 'open' for a child and family statutory assessment within a certain month, where there was an indication of extra-familial harm. We wanted to get a snapshot of the process and culture for responding to extra-familial harm in each site by looking at what happened for a small number of cases. Although a method that involves looking at a database might not sound relational, don't be fooled! Case file reviewing is an intimate and sensitive method. To use it well, you need to foster respectful and trusting relationships, both to gain access to the records and to handle what you find.

The case file review process

To begin, we asked our SPOCs to help us with access to the system. In some places, we needed IT staff to set us up with temporary passwords and other practical things. Isolating the cases of extra-familial harm for the month in question was tricky because there is not a practice of routinely recording 'extra-familial harm' on case files, so we had to find another way to identify the relevant cases. The full methodology of this exercise is documented elsewhere (Lloyd and Firmin 2020; Firmin et al 2021) and we provide a video tutorial and written guide in the Scale-Up toolkit on the Contextual Safeguarding website.

Once we had the final list, we entered the database and looked at the child and family assessments for each child. We looked at the full assessment, including written cases notes, meeting records and the narrative descriptions that justified threshold decisions. We had four main aims to guide the data collection – we wanted to understand:

- **the outcome of each assessment.** The first thing we wanted to know was how decisions were made about the severity of extra-familial harm. How did people weigh up whether a child met a 'threshold' for a certain response? These could range from 'no further action' to a child receiving a voluntary or statutory service and plan, right through to the highest level of social care intervention – a full care order.
- **the reasons given by practitioners for their decisions.** For example, if the outcome was a child being placed on a child protection plan (which is a legal process with high levels of state intervention), what were the reasons that influenced this? What

dictated if a child was considered more 'at risk' (and therefore on a different plan type) than another in the same local area?
- **the culture of the social care system.** We looked at the exact language that was written in case files, collecting short verbatim extracts to illustrate.
- **whether the system itself seemed helpful or harmful to young people.** We looked closely at what was written in the notes and reflected on whether the practices described were likely to help or cause harm (in addition to the harm that the young people might already have experienced). Young people's and parents' direct words did not feature much, but by reading the notes and being guided by evidence on what young people have said about these processes, we tried to get a sense of their perspective.

Our process was to move systematically through each case with the same set of aims and related questions, collecting information in a table.

Working with the findings from case file reviews

What did we learn? First, we gained a clear and quantifiable picture of the assessment outcomes for each site. These findings were often arresting. For example, in one site, we reviewed 43 cases of extra-familial harm. Many of the young people had experienced life-threatening levels of violence or traumatic abuse. On reviewing these, we determined that 40 cases met the statutory threshold, set out in English Law, for 'significant harm' (this determines that children receive certain social care services response; Children Act 1989). However, only eight of these cases progressed for further involvement with the children's social care department. The remaining cases (35 out of the 43) received a 'no further action' decision (Lloyd and Firmin 2020). These figures showed starkly that this social care system was failing to offer safeguarding services to children experiencing significant harm when that harm took place beyond the family home. We were working across other sites too (five in total), and our analysis revealed variations between the different sites. You can read more about the implications of this in Firmin et al (2021), but the relevance here is that this highlighted to us that these practices were not necessarily applied in the same way. This led us to ask: how did some practitioners conclude that children who have been shot or raped were not in need of welfare support?

To get at the answer to this, we needed to move beyond the numbers and look at the reasons practitioners gave for their decisions. We found that the most common explanation provided was the behaviour of the parents. Although the young people experienced harm in contexts beyond their families, what their parents were, or weren't, doing appeared to be the most important factor for determining the outcome. What's more, practitioners did not seem conscious of the fact that they were routinely closing cases for children who experienced harm in community settings on the basis that their homes were safe, despite the former being the overt reason given for opening a case. The task of ensuring that parents are 'appropriate' was so ingrained in the culture of the system that practitioners could not see that some children experiencing significant harm were being progressed while others were not, based on the context in which the harm took place.

It was only through the process of our analysis that these patterns became clear. Once we had seen these patterns, we conducted a closer analysis of the words used in the case files to get a sense of what might be happening at a deeper level that could help explain what was going on. As experienced researchers and practitioners, we knew that looking at case files could be difficult, but this did not protect us from how upsetting it was to look closely at the language used in case files. We tried to always have a member of the team available to speak to during and afterwards, for support.

To give you a sense of why this process was so arresting, we've decided to include some (anonymised) extracts, but before you read them, be aware that the content is graphic and distressing. The first is taken from a case file of a 12-year-old girl. She was referred to another agency because it was decided there was no role for children's social care in her case:

CASE FILE NOTES
[Girl's name] stated that she knew it was wrong to have sex and that she did not feel comfortable having sex but

did not say no. I am concerned that [girl's name] went into the house with a group of unknown boys and put herself at risk. Although speaking with [girl's name], she has stated that she regrets having sex, I feel that [girl's name] does not have the confidence and lacks self-esteem in herself to make her own decisions and feel that she may put herself at risk in the future.

In another case, two 15-year-old boys were open for assessment due to an allegation of rape:

CASE FILE NOTES
Referral received from the police stating that [boy's name] and another male young person have been arrested for allegation of raping a child under the age of 16. It was alleged that [boy's name]'s friend raped a 14-year-old female child whilst [boy's name] was present holding her hand. [Boy's name] did not step in to assist the victim and did not seek support afterwards. In fact, [boy's name] also engaged in some sexual activity with the same girl afterwards when his friend had left.

This assessment ended in 'no further action' for the following reason:

CASE FILE NOTES
The original referral concern appears to have been a one-off, which [boy's name] in hindsight accepts was not the right thing to do. It is clear that the social worker has explored issues around consent and has recognised the need for [boy's name] to participate in direct work with Early Help Open Access around healthy relationships, potential dangers of using cannabis and safe use of the internet. It would also assist if Early Help could support [boy's name] to engage more in constructive activities to detract his mind from potentially destructive activities.

Perhaps, like us, you are feeling angry, upset, confused. The harm is hard enough to read about, but this is compounded and intensified by how it is written about by professionals. Once we had overcome our initial shock, we started to ask: what kind of organisational culture enables a practitioner to describe the rape of a 12-year-old as 'putting herself at risk'? The fact that sex with a child under 13 is 'statutory rape' is somehow overlooked. How would it feel to be the victim of a rape by two people and be told that it was a 'one-off' and therefore no response was offered? Why do these practitioners effectively 'blame' the person who has been assaulted for the harm they experienced?

It is important to say that we were not seeking to identify 'bad' practitioners, but looking for patterns and how these patterns could be explained. To do this, we focused on the outcome and then used the descriptions to build a picture of the local culture and processes that might explain the outcome. Contextual Safeguarding is founded on the understanding that young people's actions and behaviour is influenced by the context in which they take place. This foundation shaped our approach to case file review, shifting our focus onto the context – the organisational culture and system – and away from individual practitioners. We soon began to get a sense of the culture around decision-making processes, which we deepened with information we'd gained through other methods, to look at the organisational practice on a wider scale. In Figure 3.1, you can see how we thought about different 'levels' of the system, starting with decisions made around individual cases and then moving to thinking about how local policies, practices and so on might be influencing these decisions. Finally, we thought about the wider organisation and what might be influencing factors at this level, including national policy.

To help us with the task of finding patterns, we used a set of questions to reflect on each stage of the system – these are also shown in Figure 3.1. The questions helped us to avoid blaming individual practitioners as 'bad apples' and consider forces such as social structures and collective anxieties. For example, we thought about how structures such as sexism, racism or classism influenced what was happening. In the second case file extract shown earlier, it appeared the boys came from middle-class families, and this seemed to influence decision making. In other cases, it was clear that different characteristics influenced responses – for example, when autistic children were harmed, they were described as

Figure 3.1: Case file review system questions

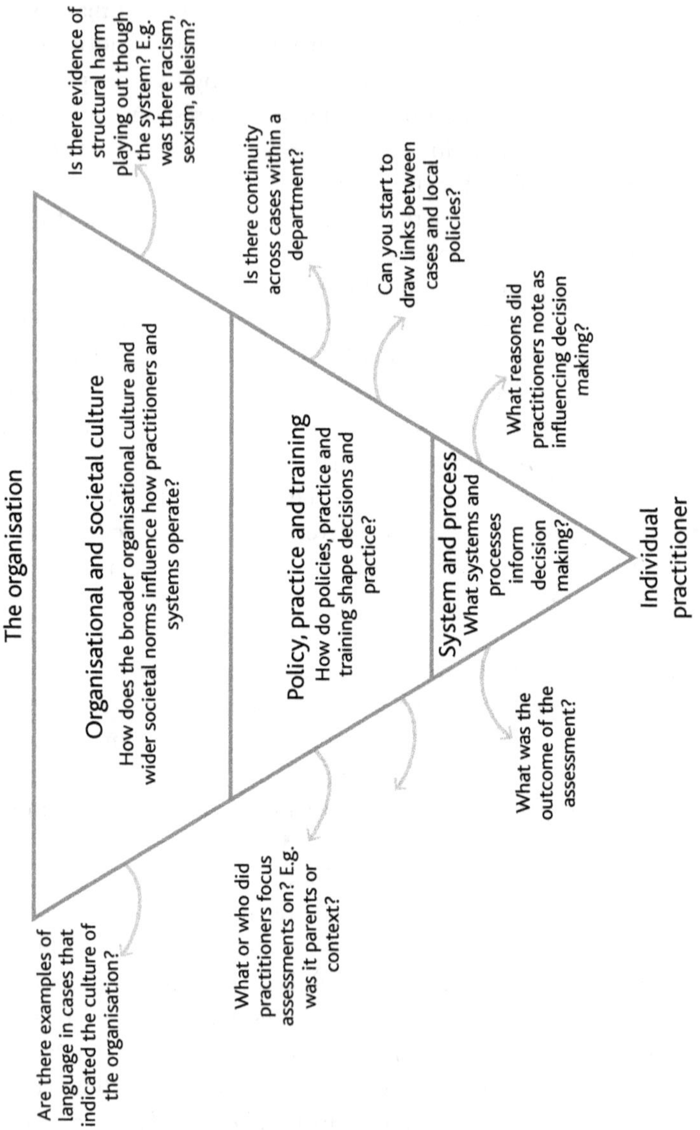

The organisation

Organisational and societal culture
How does the broader organisational culture and wider societal norms influence how practitioners and systems operate?

- Are there examples of language in cases that indicated the culture of the organisation?
- Is there evidence of structural harm playing out though the system? E.g. was there racism, sexism, ableism?

Policy, practice and training
How do policies, practice and training shape decisions and practice?

- What or who did practitioners focus assessments on? E.g. was it parents or context?
- Is there continuity across cases within a department?
- Can you start to draw links between cases and local policies?

System and process
What systems and processes inform decision making?

- What was the outcome of the assessment?
- What reasons did practitioners note as influencing decision making?

Individual practitioner

'compliant', or when Black children were harmed, the language of 'gangs' was used. But using a set of questions helped us to understand the layers of influence impacting decisions in each site.

> **Exercise 3.1: Case file review**
>
> - Create your own figure based on Figure 3.1. Make a triangle and separate it into different levels of the system. You can use ours or make your own.
> - Annotate your figure with questions you can ask when reviewing case files that would allow you to understand how the system operates in relation to the changes you are seeking to make.
> - Think about how/if case files can help you answer your questions. Where would be a good place to start?

Preparing for case review

We end this section on case file review with an overview of things to consider in preparation. First, think about how you will share your findings and who you will share them with. Also think about what processes are in place to enable the site to respond to your findings. We had pre-agreed meetings to review system change, at which we formally shared our findings. Importantly, this was underpinned by trusted relationships with leaders who were open to reflecting with us on our findings (explored in Chapter 7), which is very important if your findings include aspects that are hard to face. Second, consider the practical elements carefully. Early on, speak to data processors to find out what information they hold that can to support you to define the parameters of the cases you want to review. When it comes to the actual reviewing, we mostly did this while visiting a site, accompanied by a practitioner who could answer questions about terminology and access. Finally, make sure your notes are recorded confidentially and anonymously. Focus on quality over quantity and be very cautious about how much detail is documented.

> **Exercise 3.2: Understanding culture**
>
> - When reading case files, take notes on extracts and language that help you answer the questions from Exercise 3.1.
>   1. Is there particular language or phrasing that stands out?
>   2. What does the language tell you about how the problem is viewed or what/who is thought to be to blame?
> - Is there evidence of structural harm (that is, harm related to how groups in society are structured – racism, sexism and so on)?
> - What might a young person/patient/service user think if they saw these notes?

Reciprocal methods

When we began our work with sites, we secretly wished that practitioners would tell us everything we needed to know while facilitating access to all information and *never* asking for feedback until we were good and ready. Of course, this is wholly unrealistic! And even if it were, it would have been counterproductive to forming the sorts of trusting relationships that facilitate significant system change. We chose embedded research because what we really wanted was to build trust and intimacy with people in their professional lives, not to extract information from them. But first we needed to grapple with ethical questions about who held the power, who the relationships were 'for' and on what basis we were asking people and organisations to trust us. Ann Oakley (1993), writing about interviewing women for research, wrote that there can be 'no intimacy without reciprocity'. Later, she reflected on how researchers hold power over those they interview if the information flows only one way – from the person being interviewed to the interviewer (Oakley 2016). Historically, ideas about research as a detached, scientific process and researchers as 'objective' were all part of creating this sense of power imbalance. Thanks to the work of feminist researchers like Oakley and others (for example, McDowell 1992; Ahmed

2000; Westmarland 2001; Ozkazanc-Pan 2012), we now have well-established critiques of research being 'objective' and more opportunity for varied and subjective inquiries into the nature of people's experiences. Yet who holds power within research processes remains a live debate within research ethics (Dowling 2005). Research is still dominated by methods that prioritise data collection over participant welfare – described by Menzies as parachute research, because it involves '"parachuting" in, grabbing data, and immediately leaving' (Menzies, quoted in Tobias et al 2013, p 131).

Oakley (1993) understood that when researchers ask people to divulge personal experiences and opinions, this creates a power imbalance, and to mitigate this, the researcher needs to give something back. Our work similarly involves organisational systems divulging (often via individuals) their professional practices in a way that is inherently vulnerable to a power imbalance involving the scrutinising researcher and scrutinised system. So it became obvious to us that 'giving back' should be central to our approach, both in how we conducted interpersonal relationships – being 'ordinary', sharing ourselves, being interested in people – and in how we set up and conducted the research – making sure we didn't hold all the power and be the only ones to benefit from the process. Building on Tobias et al's (2013) work on reciprocity in their research with Indigenous communities, we wanted our approach to be characterised by honesty, humility and ongoing attempts to equalise power within and beyond the formal research process. Our work was also inspired by the long tradition within action research and participatory research of sharing power, pluralising knowledge and creating change (McIntyre 2007). This led us to a reciprocal mindset – being open to doing embedded system change in a way that reflected real life and responding to requests if they seemed possible and appropriate. Table 3.1 outlines some examples of power-sharing opportunities from our own experiences and broader literature.

This sort of process is in constant flux – we definitely don't always get it 'right', but we are committed to reflecting and learning. We recommend having a flexible approach within a broad set of clear parameters for what you are able to do, using Table 3.1 to guide your own experiences as they arise. To give you more of

Table 3.1: Power-sharing opportunities

Focus	Types of power-sharing	Specific examples from our work	How this mitigates power
Interpersonal	Doing favours, helping people out (even if not related to the project plan) and 'fitting in'.	Engaging with the social norms of the organisation, such as style of dress and wearing lanyards. Going to social gatherings, such as a leaving lunch. Being thoughtful about how you leave the organisation, saying goodbye, thanking people, talking about your own feelings about the research ending.	Being 'ordinary' helps to build relationships and avoid a sense that you are aloof, scrutinising observer. Tending to people's feelings (including our own) about what it's like to leave can equalise things and make it less like you have 'parachuted' in.
Practice	Being receptive to how practitioners need to be reassured and get feedback in different ways.	Reviewing changes to a policy document and giving feedback in a sensitive way. Spending time after a meeting to reflect on how it went.	Researchers are not the only ones in control of when feedback happens. Having regular, informal conversations about feedback avoids people being shocked, surprised or shamed in formal opportunities for sharing feedback.
Organisation	Contributing to the organisation's need to build its reputation.	Providing a statement about how the area has been an important partner in helping us to develop our work, which staff can include as part of a presentation to a senior panel.	This provides a way of giving back that acknowledges the reality that sites (and researchers) operate in a context of performance and lightens the burden of this.

a sense of what we mean, we share two examples of reciprocal methods that allowed us to 'give back' to sites: consultation and supporting learning and development. Then we consider how to respond to off-plan requests.

Consultation

Throughout our project, and increasingly as we got to know people in sites, we were asked to give advice and feedback. Take the following two examples:

- Rachael had been observing a two-hour online multi-agency meeting to discuss creating safety in a community location. A social worker was chairing, but there were lots of other people on the call, including the police, data analysts, school, drugs services and voluntary sector partners. It was hard to follow what was being said and write things down, especially as they were talking about a place Rachael had never been to and using acronyms and referring to past events unfamiliar to her. She hoped she wasn't coming across as too stern, silently writing things down. The police took a lead in the meeting, and some of the actions and things that were said troubled her. As the meeting drew to a close, she looked forward to digesting what had been said and getting away from the screen. But as everyone was logging off, the chair said, 'Rachael, can you stay for a chat?' She wondered, in her tired state, how she could (1) be helpful, (2) not draw things out too long and (3) be true to what she'd thought. (Research reflection)
- Jenny was sitting in one site when an enthusiastic professional mentioned that they had done work on their assessment framework to make it align with Contextual Safeguarding. They asked if Jenny would have a look and give her advice. Jenny said that she could, assuming this is something she could discuss with the research team. However, within two minutes the professional had sent an email to Jenny with the changes and was standing by, hoping she could give feedback as she stood there. (Research reflection)

These situations can be challenging for a researcher. They often put us on the spot, as we haven't had time to process changes; we may feel underqualified (like in the story in the opening of this chapter) or may have something delicate to say. Despite this, we decided to overcome our worries about inadequacy and unpreparedness and, instead, be open to these sorts of interactions, framing them less around 'giving advice' and more around conversational 'consultation'. Despite our initial misgivings, consultation is now an integral part of our way of doing embedded research and system change. This is because it: helps build 'ordinary' relations; gives us an insight into the concerns of the those leading and doing the change work; gives us a chance to partner with sites to make change happen; and means that people have an idea of what will be shared in formal feedback sessions so that they are prepared.

As mentioned earlier, even postmodern, qualitative researchers who reject positivist ideas can find themselves longing to be 'neutral', taking notes silently and never giving an opinion. We soon did away with this fantasy! To create real-life system change, we needed to foster reciprocity and 'ordinary' relations. So, where possible, we responded to requests meaningfully. We realised that its completely normal to be asked your opinion on the changes being made. Likewise, if you're doing embedded research, its ordinary to be interested in what an outsider thinks about what they are seeing. Sometimes, we'd say directly what we thought, taking care to be clear on the limits of our expertise. Other times, we'd respond with a question, being curious about the things that were concerning the person coming to us and opening up a reflective conversation as a response.

How we responded depended on many things, including the motivation behind the request. Reflecting on this helped us to acknowledge the reasons why someone was asking for help or feedback, which might be:

- seeking validation about whether they are on track;
- hoping for tangible outputs from researchers (that is, wording for a new policy);
- wanting to get an 'expert' opinion;
- trying to build momentum around something and gain support;

- aiming to get an outsider's view on something;
- wanting to feel less worried about something through sharing it.

We recommend using 'handover notes' (Chapter 2) to document consultation activities, even if this is a few words of advice after a meeting. Also, if there are written documents, we recommend saving versions that evidence changes, for reflecting on later.

Supporting learning and development

There were many times when we were asked to contribute to learning and development activities that only slightly related to our project. A typical example is being asked to attend/present at a meeting that was tangentially related to our own project for the purposes of supporting learning in the site. At first, we were frustrated about the thought of giving large amounts of time to activities that did not support the work we were doing. But, as with consultation, these activities had benefits such as improving relationships, making impact and giving us a broader understanding of the organisation. Certainly, we urge you not to dismiss these activities on the basis that they are 'not research'. Providing training, for example, may not traditionally be seen as a research activity, but it is an everyday part of professional life and part of how systems change. If we hold specialist knowledge and skills which we can exchange as part of our research, it makes sense to be open to this as a way to engage with sites and create impact.

Negotiating how to respond to 'off-plan' requests

To engage in reciprocal methods, we need to be able to work with ambiguity. This sort of work asks us to be flexible enough to balance being relational with getting practical and impactful outcomes and to know how and when to draw boundaries around our own work and time. Spend time reflecting on your relationships with your 'participants', or people involved in your research. If you have a team, set aside time to do this together, and if you don't have a team, try to create what you need while maintaining the confidentiality of the work.

Ask yourself what you could gain or lose from agreeing to a request and how your response relates to the wider work you're there to do. Another important consideration is to see requests within the context of structural differences. For example, although we take an open approach to reciprocal methods, we also acknowledge that 'opportunities' are often not equally distributed. As with any working environment, the type of work we are asked to do and our ability to negotiate this will intersect with our identity and social construction as individuals. Women in the workplace are more likely to be asked to undertake administrative or 'office housework' (Jang et al 2021), and this is even more the case for Black women (Williams and Multhaup 2018). This is complex terrain to navigate.

We are not suggesting that you treat relationships and people as a means to an end, and you're unlikely to say no to a request by a research partner on the grounds of structural bias. But it's important to know that when trying to maintain our personal and organisational boundaries, we will always have to weigh up our capacity and desires against the capacity and desires of other individuals and systems. As we explore in Chapter 9, there is a multilayered set of psychosocial processes going on, and in embedded research these are often played out through relationships, which can mean going beyond planned activities. As we explore in Part II of the book, building relationships is just as important as, if not more important than, keeping to a project plan. Adopting reciprocity as an ethical and methodological approach, even if it feels 'off plan', will create the conditions that enable impactful change to take place.

Conclusion

If you want to change systems using embedded research, you can forget the 'traditional' idea of the aloof researcher who watches and weighs up from afar! Although we often use observation to learn about how things work in a system (as explored in Chapter 2), we don't stop there. We firmly believe that real-life work is about being as 'ordinary' as possible, behaving in a way that is open. It's not about being precious or avoiding getting our hands dirty. When we open ourselves up to discursive and reciprocal methods, we are working in fluid, active and relational ways. As we saw in Chapter 2, this involves engaging with many unknowns. We don't know what new information case file reviews will bring up or how they will make us feel; we don't know the implications of being friendly and interested in people. One thing that is for certain: following this way of working opens you to a wide range of emotions, from guilt, imposter feelings and anger to excitement. Active methods spark these feelings, but they also provide containment too by allowing us to do something with and about our emotional responses. It can feel good to have the power to equalise relationships and 'give back' (like in a knowledge exchange) or to have some concrete information to work from (like in case reviews). Doing research in this way can be intense, but it is also rewarding and can lead to some surprising outcomes (explored in Chapter 8). We end again with some key pointers:

1. Expect the unexpected! It's good to negotiate your position and role at the start, but remember that this is fluid and things won't always go to plan.
2. Before you begin with active methods, make sure you have a good support network of people you can draw on to help you process your feelings.
3. If you're doing case file review, before you begin, have a clear process for sharing what you find – who, where, how and so on.
4. Forget the idea that research is only about collecting data and analysing it. The *way* you do this work will significantly impact the system you help create.
5. Regularly critically reflect with others about the balance you are striking between responsive and planned activity.
6. When you get asked to do something, always take a moment to think about what the motivation is and what could be gained or lost by agreeing. There are no hard and fast rules, but responding out of this considered reflection is better than a reluctant 'yes' or a reactive 'no'.

4

Developing a plan and making changes

Introduction

In Chapters 2 and 3, we looked at how we learnt about the children's social care system using more 'passive' methods, like observing meetings, or more active ones like case review. We devoted most of the first eight months of the four-year Scale-Up project to simply trying to understand what was going on. Then we paused, reviewed our learning, met with sites to discuss our reflections and worked with them to develop a plan for how they wanted to change their systems. This chapter describes that process.

You might think you already know broadly how your system works and what needs to change. That might be so, but for us, it has always been crucial to change systems in a way that is *contextual*. As we create systems that understand children's contexts, we want to engage with the specific and individual contexts and cultures of each organisation. We are also committed to research rigour, to going beyond initial perceptions and trying to understand at a deeper level and from multiple perspectives what is 'going on'. What leaders think is happening, what the policy document says and how people experience the system can be completely different. We saw this in a site where we had been told that a system was in place for responding to extra-familial harm, but found it was actually a 'process' held, overseen and executed by just one person. So, before we could create a plan to change the system, we needed to feed this observation back to the leaders so they could see how precarious their process really was. Without this realisation, we could have made a plan that simply loaded on more tasks for this already very hard-working woman. Instead, we worked with the site to create a plan that reflected a core contextual issue and made more sustainable change. This was not an isolated incident. Often, hidden among the meeting acronyms and titles, there was a logic that only made sense to a few. So, whether you're an external researcher or someone working within the system you're changing, you can capitalise on your position as someone stepping outside to look at an organisation and use the methods described in Chapters 2 and 3 to uncover things that it may not be possible for those working within the system to see.

But what happens next? How do plans come together? How do we use the relationships built in the 'fact-finding' phase to support making changes?

The system review process

Imagine that you're coming to the end of the fact-finding phase and have a better idea of what is going on in the system. This is the time to pause and reflect, to consolidate your learning, to feedback and sense check your findings with others in the system. We did this at a meeting called a 'system review' – a methodology created by our colleague Carlene Firmin (Contextual Safeguarding 2022a; you can find tools for conducting your own system reviews in the Scale-Up toolkit on the Contextual Safeguarding website). We held four system reviews in each site during the Scale-Up project. They punctuated the work, with the first following the initial scoping phase (approximately nine months into the project), another approximately a year later, just before piloting started (more on this later), a third halfway through the piloting stage and a final one to close the project. Each one followed the same format but with a focus specific to the project phase.

System review meetings were like 'mountain top' moments in the project – a chance to see where we'd come from and agree what the next climb would be. But the steps along the way were made up of regular research team reflective meetings, where the hard graft of analysing happened.

Reflective meetings

As well as the system review meetings, we held reflective research team meetings every other week. Depending on the stage of the project, these involved between three and five people, and they were always online due to us being geographically spread out. These spaces became very significant for shaping our learning about sites and preparing for system reviews. They helped us to 'hold' and make sense of the data we were gathering. Several researchers gathering data using embedded methods in five places produces a lot of data! Even if you are only working in one place, you might quickly become overwhelmed by the amount and type of material you generate and feel a bit lost about what to do with it. You might be familiar with analysing an interview script, but what about the notes of a meeting observation or a conversation at a desk or in a car? How can you turn this into something useful?

We certainly worried about whether the many strands of information we were collecting would become a big messy jumble of information. At the same time, we wanted to 'sit with' the complexity, not impose a structure just to feel better. Reflective meetings helped us find that middle ground, combining free-flowing space to talk about our thoughts and feelings with discussion about how our findings fitted with the overarching analytical framework of our project (based on the Contextual Safeguarding domains – see Chapter 1). Despite our demanding research itinerary, we prioritised these meetings because they gave us space to *do* work and contain our anxieties about the work.

The meetings followed the same structure each time:

1. check-in
2. site updates
3. actions
4. deep dive analysis into one site

Starting with a check-in was really important, so we could hear how everyone was feeling.

Then, during site updates, we spoke about what we'd seen over the last two weeks, hearing from each researcher on their activities. To help us remember, we used handover notes as prompts. It might be that Rachael had a great conversation while at a site and wanted to share this, or that Jenny had been to a different site and seen something upsetting and needed to debrief. Sharing feelings helped us to reflect on the work at an emotional level. We took this seriously in terms of our own wellbeing, but we also thought about what our feelings might be 'telling us' about the work in the site. For example, maybe after a conversation with someone, we'd felt overwhelmed, like an imposter or worried about whether we had got it right. So we thought about whether the person from the site had also felt overwhelmed and whether they might have 'communicated' this to us through our feelings. We held on to these type of questions, allowing them to inform how we approached our next visit.

During updates we'd refer back to our research project plan to make sure we were on track with the milestones, make any adjustments needed and then assign actions for taking forward, like who would lead on preparing for a system review in each site. After updates and actions, we ran a deep dive analysis for one site. We'd look together at the data (observation and handover notes, reflections and so on) from the last few weeks or months since the last deep dive. We systematically worked through each stage of the site's children's social care system, from their process for taking referrals to how they undertook assessments, to their planning and response processes. We wanted to understand the extent to which the system could:

- **target the context of harm** – we discussed together the extent to which sites had processes in place to allow them to address harm in an extra-familial context and, if they did, whether this was done by creating safer conditions for young people or by trying to alter their behaviour (or their parents' behaviour).
- **draw on welfare responses** – we looked at whether the processes and practice examples we'd seen in sites prioritised young people's safety and wellbeing or if they prioritised reducing crime.
- **develop meaningful partnerships** – we discussed the extent to which the partners who had influence in a context (both professional partners and those who live and work in a place) were being identified, engaged and brought into safeguarding responses.

- **produce positive outcomes** – we looked at whether sites had processes in place to measure the extent to which a context had become safer, as well as whether individual children were safer, as a result of their intervention.

We used the system review traffic light tool (available via the Scale-Up toolkit on the Contextual Safeguarding website) as a guide, indicating whether what we'd expect to see for evidence of 'red', 'amber' or 'green' practice. Table 4.1 provides a modified version of the table we used to hold our analysis, with some examples filled in (Firmin and Lloyd 2022).

A deep dive into a site started with creating a new version of this table or updating an earlier one then saving the new version to track progress over time. One person would lead the discussion and writing, going through the table section by section. For each stage, we'd discuss whether the data and notes we'd collectively gathered provided examples that were red, amber or green. So, for example, in Table 4.1, the leader might ask if anyone had collected data about the referral process within the site in question. Someone might mention that they had completed a review of this and found they mainly focused on individual children and didn't include much about the contexts in which young people spent time. The team would then consider which domain this was most relevant to (in this case, Domain 1) and if this was evidence of red, amber or green practice (in this case, it was red). This process often involved some hard thinking about how real-life practice examples fitted within the framework. It was often not a linear process: we would flit between discussing an example of data and where it fitted in the table, to working through the table section by section. It was time-consuming but extremely rewarding work, not only for analysing and ordering large amounts of data but also for containing our concerns about doing that in a rigorous and reflective way. It may sound a little abstract and complicated, but we had refined this process during our work in the London Borough of Hackney and found it to be very useful. You could use Exercise 4.1 to support you to devise a much simpler analysis framework – in fact, the simpler the better.

Table 4.1: Modified version of a 'red, amber, green' rating table

Domain	Referral	Assessment	Planning	Response
1. Target	<u>Red</u> • Case reviews highlight that child and family assessments do not consistently include information on contexts. <u>Amber</u> • Some cases of extra-familial harm are progressed and other are not, so there is a lack of clarity of threshold for cases of extra-familial harm. • There is no formal established mechanism for logging contexts in at the front door. <u>Green</u> • Front door have systems in place for referring locations and peer groups for assessment. • Referrals are being used for contexts (not just individuals) by multi-agency partners.			
2. Legislative framework				
3. Partnerships				
4. Outcomes				

Source: Adapted from Firmin and Lloyd (2022)

We continued to do deep dive analysis throughout the project. To prepare for a system review meeting, we'd review the latest table and change the colour of each cell to red, amber or green, depending on the evidence we'd gathered. This was not an exact science, but a helpful visual guide to support professionals to see where progress had been made or where more work was needed. Taking the example in Table 4.1, it is likely that the first box would be coloured amber because progress had been made though evidence of red practice was still significant. We were also conscious that although to us green didn't mean 'completed', it was possible it would be read this way, so we didn't use it often, because we wanted to keep the focus on system *change*.

> **Exercise 4.1: Analytical framework**
>
> Consider what analytical framework you could use to assess system change:
>
> - What are the key principles (like our four domains) that would help you know that the system change has been achieved?
> - What theories or ways of seeing the problem underpin your approach? Can these be converted into principles?
> - Are you assessing different parts of the system? Do the principles differ for each part?

The system review meeting

When it was time to have a system review, we asked sites to invite key professionals (both operational and strategic) to the meeting. The objectives of the system reviews were:

1. Recap the overall aims of the project, approach and timescales.
2. Focus on any specific questions related to the system.
3. Review findings from system mapping (see Exercise 2.2).
4. Develop and discuss progress against a plan and actions related to system change.

At each part of the meeting, we presented our most recent findings and provided opportunities to discuss the implications of these with sites. We prepared a set of slides to guide the meetings, but there was also space for emerging questions and reflection.

System reviews varied across the span of the project. The first focused on creating a plan for change, the second on monitoring how changes were going, the third on learning from pilots and the fourth on steps to embed change across the system. The text below is taken from a first system review slide, where we were presenting our reflections to the site following our initial system mapping work and inviting discussion about the system changes the site wanted to make:

> **NOTES FROM SYSTEM REVIEW SLIDE**
> [Site] doesn't have a discrete 'adolescent' or 'criminal exploitation' service to hold the approach and therefore more work is required following this system mapping session to identify the best structure for testing and potentially embedding (subject to pilots). Broader queries about workforce development and local ownership of the CS [Contextual Safeguarding] approach are also required as part of this; in particular:
>
> - Workforce training: the champions will play a crucial role in building workforce confidence (and sometimes addressing reluctance) to develop and buy into the approach.
> - Locality variations: Young people's experiences of extra-familial harm vary in each locality and so testing in one team may not surface replicable learning. We will likely need a champion from each locality to identify similarities and differences in need.
> - School engagement: Policing and voluntary and community sector interventions were more pronounced than school engagement during the system mapping period. More work is required with schools and educational inclusion to build them into the local approach.

The reflections from the meeting were then used to help agree the focus of the system change plan.

A brief interlude into the lives of researchers

Before looking at system change plans, we'll take a brief interlude into the working life of researchers. This is because there's a danger with these very organised-sounding processes that we forget the real-life, human, anxious people behind them. We forget that what we present here are only tools. Tools that help move the research forward but also contain our anxieties about the task and give the impression that we know what we're doing! So let's contextualise the story with some 'backstage' happenings.

At the end of year one, in the Spring of 2020, there were several significant shifts within the project. In April 2020, Rachael began overseeing a second Scale-Up project, which involved four sites in London and a team of three researchers. Around the same time, the original national Scale-Up project took on three new members of staff (bringing the total to six) and Jenny (the project lead) started a nine-month period of maternity leave. Alongside our team turbulence was the small matter of a global pandemic. Like many, we were suddenly home-schooling and dealing with bereavement and a whole host of other stresses. New team members had to be inducted entirely remotely. We were deeply aware of the challenges faced by young people, families and practitioners working in the sites, but also felt quite cut off from these, not wanting to 'get in the way', respectful of the huge additional demands that they were now facing. It was a difficult time of significant anxiety and loss.

The COVID-19 pandemic is often described as 'unprecedented' and of course it was completely unique, but we also want to recognise that any research project – whether in unprecedented times or not – will face turbulence. This is because research, especially embedded research, involves people with lives beyond work that are busy and complicated and changing. The methods we use ask a lot of those doing the work. They draw on strengths and skills developed not by sitting in front of a screen but by being in myriad relationships in and beyond work. These relationship skills form the bedrock of system change. But, using methods that rely so much on people in relationships means that there are things we can't control. Staff will go off sick; relationships will end; dogs will die. Rarely can these moments be planned for. In the words of Mary Schmich (1997; popularised in the song 'Everybody's free (to wear sunscreen)' by Baz Luhrmann): 'The real troubles in your life are apt to be things that never crossed your worried mind, the kind that blindside you at 4 pm on some idle Tuesday'. We have little practical advice to add here aside from a reminder (to ourselves as much as to you) to allow space for the things that happen on an idle Tuesday afternoon and not suppress or ignore them for the sake of a project plan. Create a culture where people know this to be true. And as you continue to read our very specific guidance on how and what we did, remember that these tools were in place to hold structure at a time where everything seemed to be changing.

System change plans

We've concentrated a great deal in this book on ways to learn about the system. But, if you are interested in system change, you're probably wondering how do you actually create change once you have an idea of what the issues are? And how do you change a whole system in a way that is methodical and not overwhelming? Our answer to these questions was a co-created, detailed plan for system change.

What to change

How does a system change plan come together? The good news is that you're unlikely to have to do this alone. Even if you do not have a large team involved in your project, try to involve a range of people who are invested in the system change so that the plan is as co-created as possible; you should include the views of people who use services, in our case young people and parents/carers.

Our approach was to create a shared site-specific initial plan during the first system review in response to our initial findings (scoping and red, amber, green rating). We hung large sheets of flip chart paper on the wall, one each for referral, assessment, planning and response. Moving through each stage, we asked professionals to say what needed to change in response to the challenges and strengths already discussed. We then asked the meeting to name people or teams that would lead that change. After the meeting, as a way to keep track of progress, we converted the information into a project plan with timelines, actions and people responsible. The idea was that the SPOC would lead the site in holding responsibility for making the changes, while we would research if and how these changes were working. In theory, we wanted sites to 'own' their own plans, and this is something we often discussed during system reviews and afterwards. In practice, we had varied success with sites owning system change plans. Only in one site did the SPOC take real ownership of the plan and see it as their task to check progress and keep it updated. In other places, despite regular negotiation, it seemed that sites felt that the plan was owned by the research team and they were reporting progress to us. In one site, once it had been made, we're not sure they thought about the plan at all!

Looking back, these variations didn't really impact the outcome of the research in terms of the extent to which sites were able to change their systems. But it did raise important issues around who was 'really' driving the change and setting its parameters. We wanted sites to take ownership of the plans rather than seeing themselves as accountable to us and *our* plan. Mostly, this was to do with authority and sustainability. We didn't feel we had the authority to tell already busy professionals what they should be doing, and if they saw it as *our* plan, what would happen after we left? However, by coming in as Contextual Safeguarding researchers with a predetermined – albeit broad – set of criteria for system change, based on our four domains, and then leading system review meetings and giving our feedback on their system, we had already claimed considerable authority. Implicitly, we had already set limits on the scope of the system changes that were possible. Had, for example, a site suggested that all their social care assessments of contexts should be led by the police, we would have told them that this went against Domain 2 and 'wouldn't be Contextual Safeguarding'. So, system change plans raised many questions about ownership, investment and authority and exemplified the real-life messiness of the work.

The benefits of us 'managing' the project plans were that it allowed for continuity across sites and gave us something tangible to oversee. It is likely that the question of 'who' holds the plan will vary depending on the structure and make-up of your project, but it is an important question to hold in mind when planning change, and it is probably helpful to remember that there is no perfect dynamic in terms of ownership. The question of what to change, however, will depend entirely on what you have found as result of your initial review of the system – what you have learnt from using the methods described in Chapters 2 and 3, shaped by your original aims and intentions. Perhaps you want to bring in a new practice model or improve the way the system works with a specific partner. If you have used an analytical framework (see Exercise 4.1), you should now have a way to consider where the strengths and challenges are in the system and begin to see more tangibly what you're aiming to for.

In Chapter 1, we imagined three reasons why readers might be consulting this book: they are interested in developing Contextual Safeguarding system change specifically; they are interested in system change within children's social care; and they are interested in system change within human services more broadly. For audiences interested in the latter two, the types of change you make will be determined by the aims of your project and we recommend you use your analytical framework to guide you. For those interested in Contextual Safeguarding changes, we now offer an overview of some of the specific changes that were made during the Scale-Up project. Our other audiences may wish to skip to 'Consulting with young people and parents/carers'.

Contextual Safeguarding system changes

During Scale-Up, we were interested in changing how the whole children's social care system addressed extra-familial harm, from referral stage to case closure. Table 4.2 outlines a list of the changes made by the five sites. In sharing this list, we're not saying you must do these specific things to create a system that aligns with Contextual Safeguarding. Instead, we give examples of the things that were chosen collaboratively with sites to give you an indication of the changes made. The findings and learning from many of these changes have been published in the online Scale-Up toolkit (Contextual Safeguarding 2022b).

Pilots

By the end of our first year, each site had a system change plan in place. Some of the changes suggested were small: tweaks to referral forms or discreet activities such as rolling out training. But some of the plans for change were, in many respects, quite radical. They required a complete change in how the system operated, drawing in new partners, new processes and sometimes new legal and policy frameworks. They also required substantial cultural change, but this wasn't clear to us until later on in the project.

Table 4.2: System change plans

The planned change	Actions needed to facilitate this
Referral	
When social care referrals are received, ensure those working at the front door ask questions about the context in which harm occurred. These questions are included on referral forms and able to be captured on the social care system.	• update referral forms • train front door staff • change social care computer system where needed
Make it possible to refer contexts at the front door to start a process of assessment and planning for a context (such as a school, a peer group, a neighbourhood) as opposed to for individual children and families.	• change social care computer system • create a whole pathway for contexts
Introduce written threshold documents for contexts that outline what the level of need or harm would be for a safeguarding response to a context.	• create a new threshold document template
Assessment	
Develop a process for assessing schools, locations and peer groups. This can assess harm that may be happening in a context impacting multiple young people and can form the basis of a plan for change.	• prepare policy and legal guidance • set up new meetings • train staff • introduce practice and assessment tools • create a new pathway for contexts
Develop a process for ensuring that context assessments engage young people as part of the process.	• introduce practice and assessment tools
Create changes and guidance for single assessments to support assessing contextual information relevant to individual children.	• prepare new guidance • train staff
Discuss contexts in planning meetings – for example, a multi-agency meeting to discuss instances of child sexual exploitation can also focus on contexts of concern, such as a park.	• adapt meetings • change documentation
Use context conferences in a similar way to child protection conferences – that is, to create plans for contexts when harm is significant.	• create a new pathway for contexts • set up new meetings • train chairs and partners • prepare new guidance and documentation

Table 4.2: System change plans (continued)

The planned change	Actions needed to facilitate this
Planning	
In individual planning meetings (like child protection), make reference to wider contextual work taking place by the organisation or partners.	• create a new pathway
Develop a Risk Outside the Home pathway for holding cases at child protection level where there are no concerns related to parenting.	• create a new pathway • train chairs • prepare new guidance and documentation • prepare legal advice and guidance
Response	
To address harm in contexts and create safety, develop a range of flexible responses to contexts – for example, detached youth work.	• commission • establish new partnerships
Ensure context work (as opposed to just work with individuals) is held at statutory-equivalent level.	• prepare new guidance and legal advice • prepare new documentation
Identify champions to promote Contextual Safeguarding across the site.	• train champions

To test out these more radical and complex elements of system change, in the second year of the project, each Scale-Up site ran two pilots. The aim of the pilots was to understand what the implementation of a Contextual Safeguarding approach in each local area might look like and test out specific things before deciding whether to embed them into everyday practice. Pilots allowed sites to understand, through analysing both barriers and successes, what each site might have to contend with if they rolled out the pilot at a later stage. Two pilots ran in each site over a period of 8–12 months. Some sites ran them in parallel (usually when the pilots involved different partners and had separate people leading them), and others ran them one after the other.

What to pilot?

During system reviews and in our conversations with SPOCs, we considered what the site wanted to pilot. Some had a clear idea of what they wanted to pilot and others took months to decide. Box 4.1 provides an overview of the types of pilots that sites ran.

Box 4.1: Contextual Safeguarding pilots

There were a variety of pilot types in the project. In each site, at least one pilot looked at changing the pathway (for example, the meeting structures, processes and decision-making thresholds) for individual children and for contexts themselves. However, as the most complex and novel part of the work was making contexts safer for young people, most sites focused attention on pilots that tested these changes.

Pilots focused on individual children

- **Meetings** – to test a new local area pathway for multi-agency partners to plan responses to extra-familial harm. Areas developed new ways to 'move' children through the system pathway in planning meetings that involved talking about the contexts relevant for individual young people.
- **Individual pathway** – to create a pathway for individual children impacted by extra-familial harm where there are no concerns within the home. One site tested a Risk Outside the Home category within child protection conferences.

Pilots focused on contexts

- **Family group conferencing** – to test Contextual Safeguarding Community Conferences to address significant harm within a peer group, a school or a community location.
- **Location and peer assessments** – to pilot the use of social worker-led neighbourhood and peer assessments that focus on assessing and responding to harm happening in contexts, such as neighbourhoods. Pilots included addressing harm on a street, in a park and on a housing estate.
- **School assessments** – to pilot the use of social care-led schools assessments focusing on harm in a school context. Pilots included hosting school safety summits, running school community meetings and introducing processes to work alongside students to identify harm and safety.

- **Geographical intervention** – to pilot a new partnership to assess a specific local area, using social workers and youth workers, to understand whether this could be a useful approach in other places across the county.

How to pilot

Although each area ran their pilots differently, some similarities emerged. Most areas convened a small working group around each pilot. The group's first task would be to define the pilot itself and its aims. The group would prepare any relevant documentation to help get the work agreed by senior managers. We had thought our role as researchers would be mostly to observe pilots, collect data as they progressed and consider their strengths and challenges and, ultimately, to consider what the pilots meant for the broader embedding of Contextual Safeguarding in the system. In reality, we were frequently involved in discussions of what and how the pilots should run and were faced with complex questions about policy, guidance, tools and legal aspects (as you can see in the anecdote shared at the start of Chapter 3). In some sites, professionals needed training to support their involvement in the pilots. For example, Family Group Conferencing coordinators and child protection chairs needed support to understand how to chair meetings focused on contexts rather than on individuals and families. This was all new terrain that we were embarking on together, and it's fair to say we were all nervous. As we explore in Part II, we also provided emotional and relational support to professionals who were – because of us – taking leaps of faith which was often quite daunting and unsettling. The pilots involved new partners and new ways of working and thinking, and this required professionals to challenge the status quo of the dominant culture to try to change the system.

Starting to pilot often involved a bit of waiting. Waiting for the courage to galvanise, yes, but also waiting for the 'right' case or context to come up. This was what happened, for example, in the pilot to test an individual pathway (such as child protection) for children harmed outside their home. Professionals had to wait for the right combination of extra-familial harm with no parental concerns. Those developing context interventions (like building safety in a park) needed to wait until they found a context that met the (newly developed) threshold for harm in a context. Eventually, the wheels clicked into motion in all the pilots. Practitioners started trying out new things, such as going out into schools, meeting partners on streets, carrying out street-level observations of estates and engaging with groups of young people. The full picture and stories from the pilots can be found in the Scale-Up toolkit and in other published material (Owens 2023; Owens and Bradbury-Leather 2024).

Learning from pilots

The pilots were all about learning how the system could create responses to extra-familial harm that were in line with Contextual Safeguarding. The way we did that was to collect data all the way through the pilot process. This included:

- attending and contributing to planning meetings;
- reviewing documents and guidance – including older documentation and new documentation for the pilots;
- observing meetings, particularly new meetings and panels;
- case file review, including assessments undertaken for the pilots;
- interviews and focus groups with professionals during and after the pilots.

Box 4.2 outlines the questions we used when collecting and analysing data from the pilots.

Box 4.2: Contextual Safeguarding pilot questions

Implementation

- What policy and practice guidance and/or other resources are required to support implementation of the pilot?
- What existing information has been collected to support development?

Impact

- What is the impact on the system's ability to target the social conditions of abuse?

- To what degree does the pilot draw extra-familial contexts into traditional child protection and broader child welfare and safeguarding processes?
- In what ways has the pilot enabled partnerships with sectors and individuals who manage or have a reach into extra-familial settings where young people spend their time?
- What processes are in place to monitor impact on the contexts where young people are vulnerable to abuse or harm?

Engagement

- In what ways are young people, parents and carers involved?
- In what ways are local partners involved? (Partnership agencies?)
- In what ways are local businesses involved?

Implications

- What are the implications of these findings for embedding a Contextual Safeguarding system?
- What do these findings tell us about the challenges and opportunities to be addressed in future pilots?
- How is this pilot, and the resources it has created, building a Contextual Safeguarding toolkit for the site?
- Are there resources/practices developed in this pilot that are transferable to other elements of the service response?

We used the questions in Box 4.2 along with our analytic framework (based on the Contextual Safeguarding domains) to analyse the pilots. This was done collectively during reflective team meetings, and we then shared the findings at a system review meeting. After that, we worked together to consider what we had learnt for the site's wider system change project. It's worth noting, though, that we didn't wait until the system review meetings to report on our findings. Instead, we felt it important to share them first with the SPOC in a one-to-one conversation to avoid a sense of a 'big reveal' and to ameliorate any tensions in that relationship where any of the feedback felt sensitive or challenging to give or receive (you can read more on this in Chapter 7).

Consulting with young people and parents/carers

So far, we have spoken about doing research with professional practitioners to create new systems. But, of course, we need to take equally seriously the views and experiences of the people for whom the system exists – in our case, young people and parents/carers. The closer we can get to the experiences of the people who use or receive services, the better equipped we are to critically engage with what needs to change. Doing case reviews (described in Chapter 2) gave us a new and arresting window into the lives of the young people and parents/carers as they are written about in case notes. As we read, we imagined how we would feel to be the people written about in the notes. But imagining can only take you so far. Observations and conversations with practitioners are not enough to get a rounded view, especially when aiming to change systems that involve people who are already marginalised and structurally disadvantaged. But the reason why we need to do this work can also be a considerable barrier to doing it. People who have being blamed and punished, rather than supported, by services tend not to be waiting with open arms to speak to researchers. So we looked for creative ways of engaging young people and parents/carers that would be respectful and empowering. In our first project, we ran a young people's group in a community centre that met weekly with a youth worker who was part of the team. The local area around the community centre was also assessed, following several young people being harmed there. The young people's group supported the assessment by sharing their experiences and views on how the location, and the social care response, could improve.

In the Scale-Up project, for each of the sites, we linked with voluntary and community sector organisations that had established relationships with young people and parents/carers facing extra-familial harm. We then ran workshops to discuss with young people and (separately) with parents/carers their experiences of safety and harm and Contextual Safeguarding approaches. Feedback from consultations with parents/carers corroborated the findings from our case file review around the use of blaming language and the structure of services (Thornhill 2023). The conversations with young people helped us to ground our work in the core principles they said were important – trusting relationships, respect, privacy and having fun (Owens et al 2024). We also asked young people (through discussion and surveys) about the specific proposed changes to their local social care system under Contextual Safeguarding, which included peer mapping, school assessments and working with parents/carers (Millar et al 2023). We then shared the findings from this consultation with leaders during system review meetings, and this helped shape the final system design. The following is taken from a slide at a system review where we shared young people's views on a pilot to change the way schools respond to extra-familial harm:

NOTES FROM SYSTEM REVIEW SLIDES

- Young people liked the idea of a whole school approach to explore how safe all students felt at school.
- Young people thought that teachers needed support to address issues of harm in school – for example, bullying.
- Young people suggested that young people responsible for causing harm might also need help.
- Young people worried about judgement from other students if they engaged in a school assessment and intervention and wanted adults to provide a safe space.
- Young people thought that harm occurs in school in places teachers were not aware of.

Obviously, not everyone has dedicated staff to build relationships with partner organisations and set up consultation groups with young people and parents/carers. However, you can adapt this to your resources and aims using the Scale-Up toolkit of resources provided on the Contextual Safeguarding website. Remember that consultation work is time-consuming, so you need to build time into your project plan so that you can be sensitive to the pace and level of interest of the people you are hoping to engage. You should seek to create a fluid process of listening to and processing the views from multiple perspectives. There is no ideal, linear situation where you can listen to young people, then professionals and then develop a new beautiful system together. Alongside discrete consultation activities, everyone in the system change process should be constantly engaging with the questions: How are young people, parents and carers treated by this system? Are their rights being upheld? Are they being respected and dignified through these processes? Is their way of knowing and being in the world central? And they should be committed to the difficult task of shifting in response to the answers they find.

Conclusion

Changing systems is a serious business. We can't just create a plan based on a hunch and haphazardly pull out a few changes; rather, we should be systematic and methodical. At the same time, systems are fluid and subject to unexpected twists and turns. All the way through this book, we reiterate the message that you need some tools but remember they are *only* tools. Alongside them, we need reflective spaces, deep thinking, emotional processing, the building of relationships and rapport – these less visible aspects are where the real work is happening that will enable change.

We can't tell you how long you need to spend scoping out your system before starting to create a plan, but we can tell you that once you start, you are likely to be plagued by the feeling that you should get more data. This is where you need to remember that you're doing this work in a real-life context, which means moving through the process at a pace that allows you to learn and digest but which keeps the momentum going. We hope that this final chapter of Part I has given you a vision for how you can – returning to our water analogy – immerse yourself in the system and make some waves. You won't stay dry, but it is exhilarating! We end once more with some key pointers:

1. Before you start your project, decide on broad timelines, and put reflective meetings and your first system review in the diary before you begin the scoping phase.
2. Even if you are tiny team, find a core group of people with some influence and practice knowledge who will meet regularly to review the system changes and co-create a system change plan.
3. Don't get too hung up on who is 'leading' the plan – it will work out in the end.

4. Keep your pilots focused by thinking properly about the aim and the questions you want to answer.
5. Remember that pilots are not meant to be perfect; they are meant to help you learn.
6. Be open to any and all opportunities to listen to the views of people who use services, even though it might take time and be hard.

PART II

Working with relationships, emotion and culture to change children's social care systems

In the following poem, Jenny reflects on having to deliver feedback at a system review – this was based on findings from the case review data outlined in Chapter 3 involving the sexual assault of a girl by two boys at a party that received a 'no further action' decision. The 'she' referred to is the SPOC.

I know what I need to say

I'm on the train
and I'm nervous
>   *but I know what I need to say (it isn't good)*
but I want them to like me
I know what I need to say
>   *but I want them to know that I like them*

I'm in the meeting room, this is where I'm going to tell them
And it's nice
>   *but I know what I need to say (it isn't good)*
She says, 'It's the place we go when we want to impress people'
They want to impress us?
They want us to like them
>   *but I know what I need to say (it isn't good)*

I'm in the meeting room, where's her dress from?
What do I know?

    Maybe I got it wrong?
        But I know what I need to say (it isn't good)

                In my head I'm back in that place
                reading the files
part here   part there
                at the party
but in the meeting room

                He held her hand while it happened
                then he did 'it' too

                But they were 'Nice boys'
                From 'Nice families'
                No further action
                No further action

        But I know what I need to say (it isn't good)

    I'm standing in the meeting room
    and I say it isn't good

'It's not good' (don't cry now)

                No further action
                No further action

    I'm standing here
    and I'm talking (what are they thinking?)
        What do I know?
        Maybe I got it wrong?
    I want them to like me

    I'm standing here
        And I say it isn't good

Part II

I say it for her
I say it for them

I'm in the toilets afterwards
    And she sees me: 'It's not good is it?'
(It wasn't good)
    'It's good that you said it'
    'We needed to hear it'

I feel relief
    for her
    for them
        I know I needed to say it (it's good
        that I said it)

5

Emotional containment and vulnerability in the change process

Introduction

Part I has outlined how we used a range of tools to build a coherent picture of the children's social care systems we were working with. In Part II we focus in on what we learnt about the role of relationships in applied research for changing children's social care systems. Looking back, we can see that the process described in Part I was important, not only for what it helped us to learn about these systems but also for how it helped us to contain the enormity of the task. Human systems are extremely complex and unruly, in a constant state of flux. Doing things like mapping out meeting structures and reviewing case files helped us to manage our questions and feelings about the impossibility of ever really knowing or fully understanding a system like children's social care. What we realise now is that tools to understand system processes are most helpful if we treat them as keys that help us to unlock doors. They aren't an end in themselves, but a way to see things differently. These tools helped us create certainty within a context of uncertainty. The information generated from these methods is the kind of knowledge that can be exchanged. It is recognised by senior leaders and policy makers. It is considered valid and robust. But the tools also provide a means for us to build relationships with people in sites, and through this we can unlock rich information about the culture and relational dynamics of a place. This is more subtle 'data', but just as important to understand.

We should say now that this book is structured according to a false divide. We have presented our methods and tools in one part and now we turn in this part to looking at relationships, culture and emotions as if they are wholly separate things. In reality, they are deeply intertwined. Your systematic and robust framework will help you find things out and make changes, but what you find out, and how you do so, will be deeply dependent on the relationships you build, how well you tune in to emotion and how much you can engage with culture. To work on both terrains, we need, on the one hand, practical, organisational and intellectual skills and, on the other, the ability to tune in to emotional dynamics, pick up on subtle cues and build rapport and connections with people. So whereas Part I described what's going on 'above the surface', now we turn to thinking about what is going on 'below the surface'. In this chapter, we begin by looking at the relationship between ourselves and the SPOCs, and then we explore the role of emotional containment and finish by discussing building relationships online.

Why relationships matter

So why do relationships matter in applied research? Let's start with a story from the end of our first year on the Scale-Up project. One of the team had been invited to a meeting with some senior leaders in a site to discuss their proposed adolescent strategy. This sounds perfectly reasonable, but the trouble was we'd just completed several months of fact-finding activities in the site, held a system review meeting and agreed a system change plan with what we thought were the key players. At no time had we heard about an upcoming adolescent strategy. Somehow, in the neat process described in Chapter 4, we'd missed something. The result was that some key senior people (who we're calling Lesley and Jan) were out of the loop, confused and had an alternative plan. The SPOC (who we're calling Fran) thought it would be good if we could meet with the leaders and try to get them on board. Here's a reflection recorded in a handover note, written by the researcher after the meeting:

HANDOVER NOTE

There is clearly some tension between Lesley and Jan which I had not appreciated before. They had a few slightly tense exchanges between them in the meeting. At one point Jan suggested that they both do different things in terms of their strategy and then review and develop 'hybrids' of what works. This adds to the already substantial challenges of doing systems change in [site], because they are divided in their vision and methods of decision making. After the meeting I was walking to the toilets with Fran. She turned to me and said, 'Did you see the tension between them?' It was a relief to talk about it, because I'd found it pretty stressful to navigate, but it also felt weird to be a researcher and having this sort of backstage, conspiratorial chat with her. It all felt a bit messy.

This vignette highlights the complexity of our relationships in system change work. Perhaps this complexity is one of the reasons why explicit engagement with relationships can sometimes be overlooked in change programmes and innovations (for example, Fischer and Miller 2017)? It's as if we'd prefer they didn't exist. We surge forward with things like 'task and finish' groups that take little account of relationships (Ruch 2011) even though they are a ubiquitous part of life, especially when it comes to human services (Trevithick 2014). Feminist scholar Sara Ahmed (2013) argues that emotions occupy a low status because they are associated with the female, and perhaps relationships likewise are seen as trivial and not the focus of serious scientific enquiry because they have female associations (McNamara 2009). Surely, as the patriarchal voice nags: 'We can't think of how people *feel* about each other as data? What we need is hard evidence.' But if we listen to that voice, we will miss out on so much (Freiberg and Carson 2010). After all, we are working with *human* systems, not with mechanical processes. We want to give you permission to give the human centre stage in your research. This means listening to intuition, noticing feelings, observing interpersonal connections and care alongside the less comfortable elements like envy, rivalry, blame and despair (Bradbury and Lichtenstein 2000). When we focus on relationships in research, our work can be very powerful (Ruch et al 2016).

Tuning into relationships

So how do we make relationships central to system change work? You might be reassured to know that learning how to tune in to the wisdom of relationships in organisations has been something that we have learnt over time. It wasn't at the front of our minds when we began this work. As we have described, at the beginning we focused on the things that were most obviously apparent, the things that we could see: meetings and referral forms; panels and policies; and databases and other ways of processing information. In the beginning, we mapped systems. We talked with practitioners about their challenges and looked for solutions. We developed new tools to support their practice, hoping that this might change the system. But it didn't always work, and eventually it was this frustration with our own methods that led us to a deeper appreciation of how we needed to build closer relationships so that we could understand the cultural landscape of children's social care systems.

Here's a vignette about an experience like this, where we made a tool for one thing but realised later that it might be a key to something completely different:

RESEARCHER REFLECTION

In the first site, where we were developing our methods, a group of practitioners were keen to run an assessment of a context. We listened to their frustrations about not having a good form that would help them contain and shape the information they should gather for this and then weigh it up afterwards. So, as diligent researchers, we went off and produced a beautiful assessment template. It was a matrix with contexts along the top and different people (young people, adults and so on) along the side. We presented it to them. It seemed pretty straightforward to us, and we thought it would be helpful to them in moving forward with the assessment. But that's not what happened. The team found the matrix confusing and overwhelming. They didn't like how big it was. In fact, it was so big that they were unable to see the whole thing on a large screen and needed to move the screen along with a mouse. There were too many boxes, and the ones left unfilled tormented them with a sense of missing information. When the team were unable or unwilling to use the form, we were confused. It was exactly what they needed (or so we thought). We became as frustrated as they were and confused about what the problem was.

There was rich information in this exchange, but we were not tuned in to it at the time. If we had been able to use the tool as a key to understanding the relational aspects of this system, it might have led to conversations with the team about how they were feeling about the task: what was getting in the way, and why? We might have seen that the team's response to the tool reflected how impossible the project itself felt to them. We could have viewed their objection to scrolling across the screen as linked to a feeling that there was just too much information to be held. Perhaps the blank boxes were so tyrannical to the team because they represented what they did not know, which was particularly hard to bear in the context of an organisational environment where the team was being looked to for answers and expertise. And on top of that it was fiddly. These are conjectures; we did not have these conversations explicitly, but if we had, it's possible to imagine how this 'data' could have changed the focus of not only how we worked but also what we were focused on. If we had been able to find a way of talking about their feelings and our own frustrations, we might have come to a shared realisation about how, within this system, there was something less tangible obstructing us in doing this work – something that lived at a deeper level than we had been operating on up to then.

We now believe that understanding the relational landscape of an organisation, and the anxieties that underlie it, is just as important for making change as the information we glean about policies and processes. If we hope to bring about lasting change, we need to sensitise ourselves to what's going on 'beneath the surface', despite all its messiness. Alongside facts about the system, we need to excavate information about *why* things happen (or don't happen). Whether you're an external researcher coming into an organisation or already part of that system, it will serve you to pay attention to the emotional terrain, the complexity of relationships, the expectations, assumptions, norms and so on that flow around and within organisations.

> **Exercise 5.1: Getting beneath the surface**
>
> 1. Think about a system change activity you've been involved in that troubled you or stayed in your mind. Take three minutes to free-write about what happened. Free-writing means writing down your thoughts as they come to you without worrying about phrasing, grammar or style.
> 2. Read back what you have written and reflect on what might have been happening at a relational level. Here are some prompts to help:
>   - How did you feel in this situation?
>   - How do you think other people were feeling?
>   - Is it possible that some of the things that happened could have been a result of anxieties or worries that haven't been verbally expressed openly?
>   - What opportunities might there have been to engage with these feelings as part of the process?

Starting embedded research relationships well

The first thing we do when starting our research projects is meet the people involved. The first meeting is a very important threshold for the research; it's where we're trying to establish a rapport but also get a sense of whether this is going to be a place where the research is possible. Do we feel welcomed? Are we picking up on any defensiveness? Has someone been asked to be part of this research but their heart is not in it? In embedded research, the relationships we build at the start are very important. We are trying to dispel the idea that we are there to scrutinise and judge while also wanting to build the sort of trusting relationships that will allow us to stand alongside the team or organisation we are working with to consider what could be different. At the same time, we are human beings and we want to be liked ourselves, to feel comfortable in our working environment where we know very little and most people around us know a lot more about what's going on. This creates quite a complex power dynamic – which is a feature of all relationships. The people around us might worry what we think about their work, but also we need them to show us where the toilet is or let us into the kitchen if we need a drink.

Despite our best intentions, our positionalities and what people think or assume about us can put a heavy weight on how we are perceived and form relationships. One colleague described doing research that involved her sitting in someone else's office and going through case files. She was sat in the basement and was feeling quite lonely. At one point, a youth worker who she hadn't met came in to see if she was ok. They made a remark that suggested they felt relief on seeing the reality of our colleague – she did not apparently fit the stereotype of an intimidating academic researcher they had been expecting. She was 'ordinary', someone they could relate to. This reminded us about how much is going on in our minds, how much we project or imagine about each other, especially in those delicate first few weeks when we are establishing relationships. These projections can be particularly lively between the primary 'gatekeepers' in the team or site and the person leading the research. What kind of ideas do we each have in our minds about what the other person is thinking? What kind of power do we hold? How can we downplay any sense of intimidation on either side? This work is emotionally tiring.

One approach that helps with this is if the person in the researcher role takes a position of not knowing. This is of course what they need to do if they want to learn about the system. Not knowing much can work to our advantage in this situation, helping us to position other people as experts and ourselves as the ones who are there to learn from them. It is important that this is not contrived but done with respect and the desire for learning (Lloyd 2021). In Chapter 7, we talk about how we manage the position of 'expert' and how we negotiate giving feedback, but certainly at the beginning, expectations around this are less likely to be an issue. This is where the methods described in Part I can help us, because they can legitimise and systematise our enquiries. We observe and ask questions, and this helps us to find the answers but it also helps us build a relationship based on respect and trust. By making our enquiries, we are (hopefully) saying: 'We are not here to dominate you or tell you what to do. We want to learn with you about how things can change.' But building relationships is not something you can tackle head-on. We can't just go for endless coffees and lunches with the team! We are in a work setting and we need to do some work together. The important thing to remember is that this work has a dual purpose – underneath all the fact-finding, we are also hoping to create a sense of trust and connection that will support us in the complex change work to come. The following quote by Miranda Threlfall-Holmes sheds light on this idea:

> When a child asks Why? Why? Why? They are not only – or not primarily seeking information. Although their questions may be prompted by a genuine curiosity about how the world works, they are also an example of what linguists call phatic speech – that is speech designed not so much to communicate facts or exchange information, but to establish relationship. (Threlfall-Holmes 2023, p 46)

When you begin to research and support an organisation through a process of change, it will serve you well to keep these dual purposes in mind. Remember that you are there to find things out, but just as importantly you need to establish good relationships. In our approach, the relationship that was especially important was between ourselves and the SPOC in each site. Our relationships with SPOCs were pivotal for how we understood and accessed all parts of their local system. They used their cultural capital to give us access to spaces that we would never have been able to negotiate alone. They also provided a place to come back to, perhaps at the end of a day of fact-finding, to help us contextualise what we'd learnt. They gave us stability in a process that often felt confusing and overwhelming.

> **Exercise 5.2: Finding out who you know**
>
> Think about who the key people or points of contact are in the organisation you are working with. Do you have structured opportunities to meet with them? Is this prioritised? Consider what opportunities there are to build relationships beyond this.

Building emotionally containing research relationships

It's hard to underestimate the importance of having a strong and trusting relationship between a researcher and a SPOC or other key people. In our work, this was probably the most significant factor for bringing about change. We saw how generative this kind of partnership can be. We each have slightly different roles, which overlap and complement each other: the researcher has a role that is curious, supportive and critical; the SPOC takes up a position that is critical but also realistic about the system we are trying to change. The researcher is by necessity slightly removed, allowing them to see and hold on to a set of ideas, frameworks and futures. The SPOC, by being embedded in the system, can make these changes happen. Together, they navigate barriers and support each other to not be overwhelmed by them, as each might on their own.

We have worked in other projects where the focus was not on changing systems through a partnership between the researcher and the SPOC. While relationships were still very important, the focus was on observation and reporting rather than actively generating change together. In these projects, without a researcher to share the responsibility for system change, we saw that it could lead to feelings of overwhelm in local leaders, who seemed to experience the process of change as a more individual rather than a shared process, resulting in self-blame and guilt when inevitably the dreamed for change fell short of the mark (Lefevre et al 2024). In contrast, when we have taken a more involved position with a local leader, we have seen some remarkable examples of changed systems (see Chapter 8). In the following, Rachael reflects on a relationship she developed with a local leader of a Family Group Conference[1] service:

> ### RESEARCHER REFLECTION
> I remember my first meeting with Clare. The SPOC in the site had set up a meeting with her and I didn't really understand why. Clare told me about work her team were doing to use Family Group Conferences (FGCs) to address the needs of children experiencing extra-familial harm. I realised this was a person who was really getting things done in new and dynamic ways. This sparked an idea in my mind about whether Clare would be open to her team using FGC methods to address harm in a context – where a park or a shopping centre might become the focus, rather than a child and their family. She was very excited by this idea and so was I. Over the next few months, Clare and I met with a small group of her FGC practitioners many times. We got to know each other and talked over the challenges and worries that the practitioners had. I have to be honest, I wasn't sure at that stage if anything would actually happen, because, generally, moving from an idea to action in system change is the hardest thing. But to my amazement the team managed to run six community Family Group Conferences. Recently, I was talking to Clare and we reflected on how our relationship works. Clare is such an action-orientated person and I am more reflective. We talked about how I can support her and her team to think about their work and consider how it relates to the overall frameworks we're working within. I can help with making the case for why the work is valuable and needs more investment. Clare managed to get this new method off the ground, even during COVID-19, which is definitely not something I could have done. She also secured funding to carry it on when there wasn't much

---

[1] A Family Group Conference is a decision-making method based on Māori community practices. It is widely used in child protection processes in the UK to support families to develop their own plan for creating safety for a child. Its purpose is to minimise professional power and elevate the care and wisdom inherent within family networks.

local support for this. So we have very complementary skills. We have this strong sense of trust and respect for each other, and I think it's this that has really contributed to the success of the work.

As this story shows, the relationships that we have with those delivering change have the potential to be very generative. As researchers we have the opportunity within these roles to offer a space that is outside the ordinary day-to-day life of most professionals, where they can think differently about their work, and we can join them in creating a new type of system. We have found that an important element of this is offering a safe and supportive relationship. While we are not suggesting that we become like therapists, we are suggesting that there is the possibility for our relationship with local leaders and SPOCs to be emotionally containing. We have seen that when this sort of safety and stability is possible within the context of a professional relationship, it can facilitate experimentation, openness and permission to make mistakes.

A helpful framework to think about the role of relationships within complex systems is the psychosocial concept of the container/contained. This concept originated with psychoanalyst Bion (1962), who describes how a primary caregiver (in Bion's terms, a mother) enables a preverbal infant to process their strong feelings by entering a state of 'reverie'. In reverie, the carer is receiving, digesting and then 'giving back' difficult feelings to her child, helping to make these more tolerable (Waddell 2018). Within this conceptualisation, the carer's emotional and mental capacity to hold the baby's needs are part of the developmental process that helps the baby to develop their own capacity to think. These ideas have since been applied to thinking more broadly about the emotional processes going on within groups and organisations, particularly in settings where there are strong feelings to be processed, as in social care (Cooper 2018). Menzies Lyth (1960), for example, looked at what happens in an organisational setting (a hospital) that did not provide opportunities for dealing with the difficult feelings generated by work that involved coming close to suffering and pain. She found that not being provided with a space to feel and think led to those painful feelings being 'acted out' in defensive organisational behaviours, which were counterproductive to what the organisation was there to do and led to high rates of staff sickness.

This is not to suggest that we literally think of ourselves as carers and our colleagues as infants. What we are suggesting is that organisations are complex systems and that emotions are an integral part of how they form and develop. Social care is in the business of trying to ameliorate injustice, abuse and pain. As if this wasn't enough, trying to change how social care is done can be very unsettling. Very few of us welcome change and stepping out of our comfort zone. There is also a wider context of the organisational, governance and political environment within which we try to create system and cultural change, often characterised by scrutiny and competition (Schram and Silverman 2012). So when we work with a team to help them make changes, we need to have our eyes and hearts open to this reality. We need to expect that there will be strong feelings in the systems we are working with (Armstrong and Rustin 2018) – there will be resistance, fear and defensiveness, which can also play out in our relationships between ourselves and the local implementor. The learning from psychosocial concepts is that one way of avoiding this, and working with, rather than against these things, is to offer safe and emotionally containing relationships, where there can be mutual sharing of uncertainty and honest processing of feelings (Ruch 2011). Going back to the vignette about the reaction of the team to the assessment table, we can see that they may have benefited from this type of relationship, so that their experiences could have been thought about rather than expressed through resistance to the size of a form.

You might be thinking: 'Not only do you want me to tune in to emotions, but you now want me to "contain" them too – how do I do that?' The place to start is to ensure that you have methods and tools that help *you* to feel contained. Those outlined in Part I are instrumental in ensuring you feel emotionally contained and that the task of *doing* system change doesn't seem so big that your own anxiety spills out onto others. Second, methods that involve listening and hearing, particularly in systems where there isn't a lot of opportunity for this, will provide containment, so you can rely on this process happening naturally if you are genuinely interested in learning from others. Third, it is important to ensure there are formal and informal processes for giving feedback, rooted in reciprocity, kindness and rigour so that everyone is held in a safe process (described in Chapter 7). Finally, it is essential to pay attention to your own needs and opportunities for reflection and ensure that you too are supported with supervision and care.

Being 'good enough' researchers

The focus of this book is on real life and not an imagined and unobtainable ideal. This is a central principle to hold on to when thinking about building and maintaining relationships with, for example, SPOCs and local leaders. Another helpful concept based on the carer–infant relationship is the idea of the 'good enough mother' (Winnicott 1963), which is about a caregiver's ability to be responsive, empathetic and available to the needs of their baby, but acknowledges that it's not possible to do this perfectly all the time. Likewise, we can think of our relationships with SPOCs and local leaders as 'good enough'. Good enough is not about settling for something that is just ok, but about seeing that human relationships are bound to have times when we are not really attuned to each other, not always as sensitive to each other's needs. To emphasise this point, while we have had some very generative and enabling relationships, of course, we have experienced challenges, tensions and misunderstandings in relationships. Here is a short extract from our handover notes about an early experience of visiting a site:

> ### HANDOVER NOTE
> I met with the child protection chairs – [SPOC name] had organised the meeting but didn't tell any of us the purpose so it was a bit embarrassing and awkward when we met. They spoke for a long time about 'risk management' meetings (a new thing that has been set up for extra-familial cases), and they seemed annoyed that they might lose their independence and central oversight. I will speak to [SPOC name] and ask her not to set up meetings like this unless she is there.

Later, when we were hoping things would be in full swing and the communication would be flowing, we found that research partners had different priorities and were not as focused on the research as we hoped they would be. This can be especially difficult when building relationships remotely. It is not hard to read the sense of despair and frustration in the following handover note written by a member of the research team:

HANDOVER NOTE
- Emailed Steve on the 28/3/2021 no response.
- Invited to workshop – no response.
- Called on mobile – no answer. No answer machine.

Of course, we researchers are equally capable of causing frustration or even a sense of abandonment among SPOCs. In the areas we worked within, we were in some ways the 'custodians' of the idea that we were testing, the ones who proposed it as a way of working. Given how anxiety-provoking it is to change organisational systems and practices, especially in the context of work addressing harm to children, it makes sense that SPOCs might look to us for support and emotional containment. Returning to the 'good enough' idea, while there were many times when we were able to connect with SPOCs, sometimes we could not. Here, we return to the example that we used to open the book, when a child died and the SPOC in the site (who we'll call Stacey) had tried and failed to reach a researcher soon after.

HANDOVER NOTE
Stacey and I discussed recent events in [town name], where a young person has died. Stacey had tried to contact us on the day, or close to the day when it happened, but had not been able to contact us.

This incident had a big impact on us as a team. It brought into reality for us the high stakes of the work we were involved with and what it meant to try to change systems in this context. It caused us to reflect on the responsibility we held in our relationships with sites. While at one level we knew that we would never be expected to be available all the time for a SPOC, at another level we deeply regretted that Stacey had not been able to reach us on that occasion. We were moved by the fact that she had contacted us, and we wondered how it had felt not to have been able to reach us. Although we felt a sense of sadness at the event and about not being able to speak with Stacey, in another sense it showed the strength of the relationships that had formed and which continued to grow and develop after that time.

Building relationships online

We need to acknowledge the reality that the context of systems, and how relationships are formed and maintained, has changed significantly post COVID-19. In the Scale-Up project (2019–23), the transition to online working was abrupt with the onset of the pandemic. In many ways, we were helped by having already built relationships in person. However, since that time, most of our work has continued online. It seems that in children's social care at least, there has never been a return to the in-person demands of before. If you are faced with the prospect of mostly, or entirely, working online, then our advice is to prioritise relationships and the formation of these as much as you do the methods you will use to collect 'data'. You will need to work harder, you will need to schedule more debriefs, and you will need to feel comfortable taking up people's time to talk.

Conclusion

Human services work is all about working in the context of inequality, pain, trauma and loss, within a context of decades of neo-liberal ideology and austerity policies. Consequently, when you set about doing research in the way we describe in this book, using embedded relational methods, you too will experience the emotional impact of this. But working in this way can also be very enriching. By prioritising relationships within the work; you are likely to gain a new group of people with whom you can share the pain and triumphs of your shared endeavour. Perhaps it is worth mentioning here that our relationship – Jenny and Rachael's, that is – started out when Jenny (the researcher) worked in a site with Rachael (the practitioner). This relationship was formed not in the confines of system mapping or case review, but the moments in between, such as when Rachael asked Jenny if she wanted to have lunch together and accompany her in returning some library books! Find ways to prioritise relationships in your work, and not only will you reap the benefits of understanding the rich culture of a place, but you will create a network of those willing to walk alongside you to make change (and get to those important errands). The following pointers are based on the learning from this chapter:

1. Reflect on things that happen as part of the project and consider: What might be going on under the surface? What feelings might be shaping this?' For example, revisit a piece of data and reflect on the questions in Exercise 5.1.
2. When building a research plan, account for how you will form relationships and create formal and informal routes to enable this – for example, through a SPOC role.
3. Use opportunities for your own supervision and reflection. Consider how your own positionality or others' perspective of you might shape the project.
4. Explore the gaps and opportunities for the project to contain the feelings of professionals involved in the work. For example, finding out what supervision and support professionals already have will help you understand the role that reflective research spaces might have, if you introduce them.
5. Focus on being 'good enough'. Ultimately, your relationship with the local leader will not last forever – it is time limited. So the 'good enough' (i.e. not perfect) nature of this can help you both, when you come to the end of your shared task.

6

A relational approach to cultural change

Introduction

In Chapter 5, we argued that valuing relationships is fundamental to creating change in children's social care. We explored the relationship between ourselves and the key people working in sites and the role we can play in understanding the emotions that shape what happens 'beneath the surface' in systems. Ultimately however, despite being a large research team, we were very small compared to the number of sites in the project and the number of people involved in those systems. Our influence was dependent on our relationships with the SPOC, but the change that took place beyond our direct involvement was, equally, dependent on the relationships they developed within their systems. While it's true that we spent considerable time visiting sites and working directly with SPOCs and getting a good grasp of their systems, at the end of each day we left for our hotel rooms or to go home. We lived many miles away and were part of other academic organisational teams and systems. In contrast, SPOCs held the important task of integrating into their system the things that we'd discussed, planned and reflected on together. In this chapter, we look at their work and think about the relationships that SPOCs had with their own wider system, particularly exploring the way that they worked with, influenced and changed not only local structures but also local cultures.

What is culture?

Let's begin with what we mean by this intangible thing we call 'culture'. Most people wouldn't dispute its existence but would find it hard to define. Culture might be revered by system change researchers (Jones et al 2005), but you'd rarely see it as an agenda item in workplace meetings. When it comes to organisational culture, we're talking about things like the working practices, processes, behaviours and rituals, the management style and the values and beliefs (Atkinson 1990). These things are all interrelated, so the values and beliefs held by an organisation collectively are in a dynamic relationship with the way people behave – in Bourdieu's (1984) thinking, this constitutes the 'rules at play' in a particular context. Focusing on culture helps us to tune in to the complex web of relationships within an organisation and how people influence each other to create social conditions.

Organisational cultures do not change overnight, and certainly not at the behest of some plucky researchers from a fancy-sounding university. In our projects, the real work of system change was created, over time, by those people *doing the work* – the SPOCs and their colleagues. It took us a while to learn this; we did not initially see cultural change as essential to system change. The plans we carefully created, using methods outlined in Part I, focused on structural and material changes, trialling, for example, information systems, ways of accepting referrals and meeting structures. Only one of the five sites mentioned culture change in their system change plan. However, over time we began to see that another type of work was going on beneath the surface. SPOCs and other key people were busy engaging in a process of culture change, and the primary means of doing this was via relationships.

We now understand that we reify structural change and ignore cultural change at our peril. Introducing a new meeting structure, for example, may be valuable for helping us to organise our thinking and make decisions in a new way, but the *process* of creating the new meeting and the *way* the meeting happens is just as, if not more, important. While the surface activity might be all about what kind of minutes we need and who will chair, beneath the surface it's all about building relationships, influencing others, shifting attitudes – this is the place where we form the organisational culture. This beneath-the-surface work is vital to the success of embedding change in a system.

What kind of culture do we want?

Before we look at how sites used relationships to develop culture, let's think about what kind of culture we are hoping to foster. In our case, how does culture impact the work that happens with young people? In Contextual Safeguarding, we draw on the ecological theories of Bourdieu (1984) and Bronfenbrenner (1986), both of which consider how people's development, behaviour and experiences are inextricably linked to the environment in which they take place. This is about how collective attitudes and values exist within different ecosystems and re-enforce the power of some people and diminish the power of others within these systems. In our work with young people experiencing harm in their communities, we are talking about how the norms around young people's actions are influenced and interpreted and, in a broader sense, how the young people are regarded by those who have most influence. An example of this is the pervasiveness of victim-blaming narratives held by practitioners, such as the idea that children could be responsible for their own exploitation (Lloyd 2019). Through system change, we'd want to shift towards a culture which centres love and care for young people.

Our experiences of reflecting on cultural change has shown us that the local areas that do well with Contextual Safeguarding are ones where young people are thought about positively and seen as citizens and active members of society, and where their actions and behaviours are seen as 'making sense' within the context in which they happen. These traits are often not aligned with dominant societal attitudes towards young people, who occupy an ambiguous place in mainstream culture, being both envied (Vogel 1999) and vilified (Nijjar 2015). We worship youthful beauty, but criticise young people's laziness. We laugh at their naivety and confidence. They are liminal – neither children nor adults. They have sex, but we would rather not know and we definitely don't want them to have babies (Duncan 2005). They are noisy and visible. They are not economically active, and their developmental task is orientated around socialising. Meanwhile we adults graft away, earning the money and paying taxes. Black young people, gay, queer, trans and lesbian young people, young boys, young girls, young people with disabilities, non-binary young people and young people whose lives intersect several of these 'categories' and identities experience intense combinations of society's complex relationship with 'others' and particularly 'othered' youth (Phoenix 1988). This is the milieu within which we seek to change systems for young people harmed beyond their homes. These are powerful processes that exist in the affective realm, where envy, fear and guilt are transferred and manifest in the attitudes and behaviours of adults – the power-holders – towards young people.

How culture influences professional practice

Power and influence are always in flux. So it's important to recognise that cultural norms exist within complex ecosystems. When we describe a culture of professionals talking negatively about young people, blaming and shaming them for their actions, we need to understand what purpose such attitudes serve for these workers. Culture emerges out of set of circumstances; it does not just spring from nowhere. So when we try to understand what is going on in sites in terms of their culture, we do not think 'here is a group of professionals with "bad" views'. Rather, we *try* to think about the underlying reasons for cultures forming. We say 'try' because we too are human and often implicated in the cultures we're trying to identify. Research in this area has shown, however, that cultural ideas about young people's experiences of extra-familial harm impacts the responses they receive, as when myths about Black young people lead to their 'adultification' (Davis and Marsh 2022).

Although there aren't many studies that examine the link between the culture of professional organisations and outcomes for young people, we can learn from work in other disciplines. One such example is the work of Bigby et al (2015), who sought to understand the dominant cultural patterns within residential care homes for people with intellectual disabilities. They observed how staff interacted with residents in the home to understand whether there was a link between high-performing residential homes and a culture of positive regard towards residents. In their observation, they looked for examples of whether staff treated residents as 'people like us'. They found that in low-performing homes, there were multiple examples of staff treating residents as 'not like us'. Bigby et al (2015) were looking at how the power-holders upheld a culture of connecting with the common humanness between staff and residents or whether they were engaging in 'othering'.

Thinking about the culture of safeguarding services for young people affected by harm outside the home, we can reflect on the conditions that support practitioners to connect with the humanness of young people, as opposed to othering them. Despite the generally negative public perception of young people, local leaders could have considerable influence over the culture within a service area. A particular feature of extra-familial harm is professionals meeting and sharing information about young people in the name of safeguarding. This can be ethically problematic, resulting in the violation of young people's rights and creating relationships of surveillance rather than trust (Wroe and Lloyd 2020). When we spoke with young people in the Scale-Up project, one of the consistent messages was that professionals need to be aware of the power they hold when sharing information about them. In the following interview extract, a practice development manager in a schools-based pilot describes how the information-sharing culture within a multi-agency meeting was not respectful of this. They explained that:

> 'Previously some of the schools attended that meeting ... used some of the information that they'd heard at the meeting inappropriately. Although we're going to have a new chair, so obviously inevitably that might change the dynamic.'

Notably, despite admitting that there was a culture of violating young people's rights, the manager recognises that this is not inevitable and that a new chair could change 'the dynamic'. It *is* possible to shift a culture away from inappropriately sharing information about young people.

In another example, we heard how practitioners would talk in professional meetings about young people in derogatory or blaming ways. Returning to Bigby et al's (2015) study, we could say that when professionals said things like, 'well that young person has a track record' or 'the young person is choosing not to work with authorities', they were not relating to young people 'like us' but engaging in othering practices. The leaders in this site said that they saw a direct link (as in the care home study) between a culture of professionals using derogatory language to describe young people and a lack of progress in the effectiveness of their work to keep them safe. In the following quotation from a practitioner focus group, a professional describes their growing awareness that they need to collectively resist cynicism and instead think positively about what can be done:

> Even with those reoccurring [places] of concern that do have a particular name for themselves, when [those places are] raised for discussion [in meetings], we don't come across the attitude of 'it's always been like that'. It's: 'Right, well what can we do? How can we make it safer?' It's important to be really mindful of [cynicism] … because if professionals are thinking in that way, then what are those young people going to be thinking of their own communities? So obviously the more professionals are feeding back and being positive towards this, the more likelihood the young people [will engage]. It's showing that respect, isn't it?

Here, the practitioner sees that speaking positively about young people's communities even when they are not present, can influence how young people feel about where they live, making positive changes more likely. If there is a local culture in which professionals are positive and nonjudgemental about the idea of co-creating change in a community context, it ripples out to the respect they show to young people and how they engage in the work.

Exercise 6.1: Growing the culture we want

1. Think about how dominant cultures might be influencing the current system. Start by mind mapping the different cultural influences that shape the behaviours and attitudes of people in the system you want to change. Consider:

- What cultural influences shape how the people who receive the services you deliver are viewed? An example is how young people are viewed in society. Is this different for particular groups?
- What cultural influences shape professional responses to these people? These might be policies, performance management processes, wider legal frameworks or organisational cultures.
2. Think about what kind of culture you want:
- What are important underlying values for how people are treated and seen?
- How do you foster these values?

Drawing on relationships to influence culture

Only one site we worked with in the Scale-Up project had an explicit intention in their site plan to change the local culture. This was the site where young people were written about in case files using victim-blaming language (discussed in Chapter 3). As a result of the system review, which drew on evidence from case file review, we worked with this site to create a plan for changing the culture of how young people were viewed and responded to by professionals. The plan focused on developing core practice through training and addressing the use of terminology. A note attached to the plan exemplifies the working out of this process:

HANDOVER NOTE

[SPOC name] sees the approach to changing terminology, etc. to be through training champions to challenge and guide others across [site], rather than actually training large numbers of practitioners and managers. [SPOC] asked if we [Scale-Up team] could be involved in delivering some bespoke training to champions to this end. I suggested doing this in collaboration with her might be a good way to go. It would focus on the changes we would like them to champion (specifically rather than generally, as we might have done so far). I envisage this as being quite interactive, building with them on the ideas that have come out of the system review – i.e. role playing and discussion about the challenges and how to overcome these rather than a set of slides.

What we see here is a culture change strategy grounded in the idea of relationships. The SPOC very quickly decides against 'training large numbers of practitioners and managers'. She decides to focus on a small group of people – 'champions' – and work closely with them to grow a set of values and attitudes to help them guide others. Several months later, this SPOC and Rachael discussed again the way that culture change work was happening. Rachael was struck by the web of relationships that the SPOC had developed since the initial system review had taken place. Here is a note that describes this:

HANDOVER NOTE

There is a very interesting piece of work emerging around understanding the work that goes into trying to change practice towards Contextual Safeguarding. [SPOC name] talked about the chairs of the [extra-familial harm meeting] feeling 'put out' and her having to do a lot of 'stroking', 'soothing', 'hugging', laying the foundations in order to slowly change people's viewpoint and practice. She talked about the process being one that involves starting with 'drinks and nibbles' before eventually you can get to the stage of a full meal. It involves lots of negotiation and is very time-consuming – 'we have to work at their pace', she said.

At this time, we as a research team were developing and holding a complex set of relationships with SPOCs across five sites, which we were travelling to on a fortnightly basis. Our ability to influence beyond the SPOC was minimal. As the project unfolded in this site, we reflected with local leaders about the cultural aspect of the work. We learnt that the ability to change culture was deeply linked to the idea of organisations as relational systems. We can see this in the previous extract, which refers to the language of 'soothing' and 'stroking', which contrasts with the idea of confrontation or making a persuasive argument. The

SPOC uses a dinner party metaphor, comparing culture change to a process of inviting people first for a 'drinks and nibbles'. Thinking more broadly, we were also struck how this analogy about the local practice culture was in keeping with the wider social culture of this area, where having drinks and nibbles and dinner parties – arguably traditionally middle-class, white, English activities – might be expected and familiar to the people who live in that part of the world, which, of the five sites, was the most affluent socioeconomic area. The metaphor of eating is particularly helpful as a way to understand the role of culture, because, in the same way that food is taken in and becomes part of us through myriad biological processes, so too do attitudes and ideas become part of the way that people talk and behave. This is not about getting people to parrot by rote a certain language and techniques, but creating a sustained and owned set of shared norms and practices, underpinned by values, attitudes, feelings and ideas.

As a small research team, we looked for how we could harness the way that cultural change happens through people influencing one another. At the start of the project, the research team led a five-day training course on Contextual Safeguarding. Each site was asked to nominate five 'practice champions' to attend the training, the aim being that they would be responsible for championing Contextual Safeguarding in their sites. We wanted to provide these champions with knowledge of the Contextual Safeguarding framework and, perhaps more importantly, its underlying values and ethics, which were key to the types of changes we wanted to see. It was also, of course, an excellent way for us to form relationships within and across the sites.

Exercise 6.2: Relationships of influence

Map out key people and partners who play influential roles.

- What opportunities do you have to engage them in the process of culture change?
- Are there formal and informal opportunities for engaging them?

Parallel processes within systems

If we understand culture to be hugely influential in how social care systems address harm to young people and we agree that the culture we want is one that values, respects and cares for young people, what does this mean for how we go about changing social care systems? The concept of 'parallel processes' is helpful here (Moore 2006). Developed from work in neurobiology and child development, this theory holds that processes within systems parallel one another. This means that what happens at a practice or system level can trickle down or be 'paralleled' in how young people and families are responded to by professionals working in those systems. In short, if young people are being shown a lack of care by professionals, it's quite possible that those professionals work in systems devoid of care.

The idea of parallel systems is less about a set of practices being taught and more about *experiencing* something that you integrate and replicate with others. Thinking about child development, Moore (2006) describes how the quality of the relational experiences staff have with their managers is mirrored in the quality of relationships they have with people who use services (in Moore's case, parents). If this is true, then it means that culture change necessarily involves paying close attention to not only *what* is championed but also *how* it is championed. When the SPOC in the previous extract talks about inviting people to 'drinks and nibbles', she is describing giving people an experience of engagement that is consensual, enjoyable and fun – exactly the sort of experience we want for young people who face harm in their communities. She is hoping to create a parallel effect. While she was being playful in her language, she was also telling us something very important about her engagement with cultural change.

Providing a consistent relational experience across an organisation as a means of creating a culture is time-consuming work. We saw other examples of this parallel work in very different sites. In one area where there was already a foundation of established networks of positive relationships, the process of innovation happened much quicker, with teams of youth workers and social workers being engaged in direct practice very early in the project. This provided the SPOC at this site (who we call Julie below) with opportunities for directly influencing the team culture through leading by example. We heard about one occasion when this involved her stepping out of her managerial role to get involved in direct work with young people, described to us by Julie's manager in an interview:

> And then there was one night then, when the youth workers were down there, and somebody had been selling vapes which had some dodgy stuff in it, and the young people were dropping like flies. So, Julie was on call that night and the youth workers rang to say that they were struggling, they didn't know what to do. And Julie actually went down to assist them, because they felt that they were out of their depth with what was going on. So they phoned for an ambulance, the police attended, and they stayed there until all of the young people had either been collected by their parents or gone off in the ambulance. So, I think it was testament to the fact that, you know ... they really wanted to make sure these young people were safe.

By acting in this way, Julie is contributing to a practice culture where young people and their parents are treated with care and kindness. She's showing them that this work is not about creating distance between workers and young people – something we have seen happen in other places (Lefevre et al 2024). Rather, she is involved in building and creating a culture through relationships that is characterised by human connection. She shows her team that creating safety for young people in their communities is marked by a steely commitment to compassionate practice. In entering the 'field' (rather than directing her team over the phone), this SPOC not only shows more junior workers an approach that they can replicate, she gives her team an *experience* of what it means to be cared for themselves, to have *their* needs as workers taken seriously when they ask for help from her.

The fact that the previous quotation was from Julie's manager also tells us something about the isomorphic layers of reciprocal compassion and care that are being woven through this local culture. Her manager immediately recognises this as an example of practice to be proud of. Yet, it's also not hard to imagine the possibility that in another place, another children's service, a manager could reprimand her junior for having a lack of boundaries and for 'acting down'. But in this place, these types of relational and caring acts are in keeping with a shared culture of fostering respectful connection and commitment to young people. It is within this culture that the youth workers felt able to ask for support rather than struggling alone and feeling 'out of their depth', fearful of being judged as unable to do their work. They were able to show some vulnerability within a local culture where this is accepted and held with compassion rather than seen as a weakness. Through this example we saw how an ethics of care gave the work in this site such energy and success.

The parallel processes between practice systems and young people and families are not the only places we can see this phenomenon. These processes are evident in many organisations, and for us it is important to recognise how they can be played out between research teams or those 'doing' system change and those working in the systems that are being changed. Maybe you are coming to this book as someone more junior who feels they have little influence over your own organisational culture (but certainly can feel the sharp end of its influence). Or perhaps you are someone more senior who has some power over what and how the work is done. Either way, it is important to be sensitive to how your own organisational culture might seep into your work with others. In our own team, we have worked very hard to develop an ethics of care and compassion for one another, to maintain boundaries around our work and hold the bigger picture in mind – not micromanaging or getting caught up in the seemingly endless 'urgency' of tasks. None of this is easy in a neoliberal environment that prioritises outputs and impact but is increasingly insecure and volatile (Trevithick 2014). Much of this work has been made possible through frequent and valued reflective spaces (as in Chapter 4) and, ultimately, by taking a humane and caring approach to working with others ('off stage', we actually refer to this as the practice of 'not being a dick').

Fostering empathy

At its best a culture that was conducive to delivering Contextual Safeguarding's aims was characterised by leaders who fostered relationships of respect, trust and equality between each other and between adults and young people. As we have explored, this was about how they conducted their day-to-day interactions, but it was also about the policy decisions they made that could support this kind of culture developing. Local leaders could make decisions about resources that would support relationships to develop between adults and young people. We came across an example of this when we were involved in researching a pilot in a school. We learnt that young people and staff had started sitting together to eat. This was not by chance, but rather because leaders in the school had previously realised that there was a lack of mutual connection and relationships between staff and young people. While some might have shrugged their shoulders and seen this as regrettable but inevitable, the school leadership, in conversation with colleagues from social care, understood that this lack of connection was contributing to harmful social conditions in the school and undermining young people's safety – particularly some young people from a minoritised ethnic background. This led to the plan to enable staff and students to eat together, which included resourcing new facilities to support this, such as using a new kitchen, and providing a budget for tasty food. This example highlights how local leaders were strategic in their decisions to create infrastructures that would support a culture of relationships of care, respect and trust to develop. It contrasts with a decision in another school in the area, where a lack of funds for professional translators to assist with parent–teacher communication contributed to the disenfranchisement of some families and undermined opportunities for a culture of connection and care.

Returning to the work of Bigby et al (2015), who explored how culture in a residential care home impacted the outcomes of the work, we can see that there was a link between a local culture of empathetic connection with young people and the ability of a site to advance their work in Contextual Safeguarding. Bigby et al's (2015) work discussed how policy changes over three decades or more led to a shift in how people with intellectual disabilities are seen – as human beings, as having 'humanness'. At the local level, however, the authors are clear that this culture did not spring up spontaneously but was the result of careful and deliberate action:

> Achieving a positive regard for residents was not serendipitous in these houses, but carefully planned and reinforced. Organizational policies and procedures played a part in producing and reproducing a culture of positive regard by regulating entry, ensuring newer staff saw good practice being modelled, the explicit translation of values into expected actions and reinforcement of this through strong aligned leadership for the day-to-day work of staff. Explicit translation of policy into action avoided the dangers of leaving interpretation and policy implementation to front line staff, which is common in disability services. (Bigby et al 2015, p 291)

Thinking about our focus on young people who face harm in communities, we are a long way from this situation of having a consensus at policy level on how to relate to young people. Young people can be held responsible for crimes from ten years old, feeding into a narrative that certain children have a menacing presence, as seen in the rise of public fears about street youth 'gangs' (Young et al 2014). Alternatively, when not depicted as perpetrators, young people are treated as making foolish and self-defeating 'choices', as seen in the language of behaviour change approaches (Swirak 2016). Despite these strong national narratives, in the Scale-Up project we saw that in some local areas where leaders have a degree of autonomy and control and where there is a fairly stable workforce, it is possible to foster a strong culture of care and respect towards young people.

Bigby et al (2015) looked at cultures of 'positive regard', which involved examining whether staff treated people as if they were 'people like us' or 'people not like us'. How could we use this idea to think about our current ways of regarding young people who face harm in their communities? What characterises the behaviour and talk of practitioners? Drawing on Bigby et al's work, we argue that the idea of positive regard within cultures of respect and care for young people facing extra-familial harm, are different from cultures that inform the relationship between residential staff and adults with intellectual disabilities. Our research suggests that when it comes to working with young people facing harm in their communities, we need to expand the idea of 'like us' or 'not like us'. When we analysed our conversations with professionals about how they fostered a culture of positive regard towards young people we saw two forms of empathetic connection being drawn upon: first, [a process of] trying to remember what it was like to be young themselves, which we could call 'like I was'; and, second, trying to imagine that this young person could be a child of their own, which we could term 'like our children'. In those sites and projects where there was a positive regard for young people, we saw many examples of 'like I was' and 'like our children' talk, behaviour and attitudes being drawn on to advance a positive culture towards young people. We are not saying that young people should only be seen and valued through what we can relate to and have experienced in our personal lives; that would result in a limited form of empathy that is only based on our ability to imagine those like us. But the 'like us' approach can be a useful device for encouraging empathy in others. This is only needed within cultures that constantly override the human dignity and worth of certain young people. Really, we want cultures that value young people's inherent humanness, rather than needing to be fostered through drawing on a shared connection.

Conclusion

A phrase often quoted in business consultancy is 'culture eats strategy for breakfast' (Guley and Reznik 2019). You might have the best plan and tools to create system change, you might have the most beautiful project plan and well-organised set of research methods – but they will do nothing for you if you don't focus on understanding the culture of the organisations you are working within. We have seen social care cultures where professionals are passionately engaged in work that cares about young people and tries to promote this culture among others. We have also worked in sites that are too preoccupied with tackling crime to stop and think about what it is that young people really need. There is nothing easy about changing the culture of an organisation, and you may never really achieve this. However, it is essential that you are aware of how the culture of where you are working operates and that you focus on forming relationships that allow you to engage in the lengthy work of culture change. Looking back, we would have made culture change a much more explicit feature of sites' system change plans and prioritised this as part of the language of system change. Here are pointers based on learning from this chapter:

1. Think about what culture you want to create? What are the dominant narratives that dictate how people are seen and responded to in your system?
2. Find examples that show how people are viewed by professionals in the system. Are they treated as people 'like us' or 'not like us'?
3. Consider what and who in your site is engaged in culture change work. What can you learn from their approach?
4. Reflect on different parallel processes that might be happening in your site. How is this mirrored between yourself or your research team and professionals, and between professionals and those in receipt of services?
5. If changing the culture of an organisation seems 'too big', think about how you can influence the culture in your own work and among those around you.

7

Giving feedback on 'bad practice'

Introduction

Introducing changes into organisations, especially in human service organisations, is complex and messy work. So far in this book, we have argued that such work is greatly enriched when we build strong bonds of trust between those involved in leading the work (like a researcher) and those involved in delivering the work (like a local team). But, of course, relationships in real-life system change, as in any part of life, are not always harmonious. The researcher–organisation relationship can come under strain. In Chapter 5, we touched briefly on how there might inevitably be different priorities or misunderstandings. In this chapter, we go beyond this more everyday kind of misalignment to reflect on how we act when there is deeper dissonance between the researcher and the organisation undergoing change. We will think about what happens when researchers, in their efforts to understand a system, encounter practice that troubles them, that stands out as particularly problematic, ethically troubling and even upsetting. How do we make sense of these experiences? How can we share them in a way that is helpful and leads to change rather than shaming and causing defensiveness?

When we decided to first engage in research in children's social care, we did so somewhat naively, unaware of the emotional cost of what lay ahead. We loved the sound of being embedded researchers and immersing ourselves in the practices and cultures of safeguarding systems. We thought it would be tough – we'd both been exposed through our work to the awful things that young people experience. However, when it came to it, while it is never easy to hear about the interpersonal violence and harm experienced by children through exploitation and violence, what affected us more was hearing and witnessing harm and systemic violence to children from the very systems and practices that are designed to keep children safe (Wroe 2022). There is a kind of ethical pain associated with this that is often hard to bear (Reynolds 2011). Here we are, guests in an organisation, grateful for their support in gaining access to their files, wanting to build collaborative relationships of trust and partnerships that build shared ways forward. We know how vulnerable it is to invite researchers in to watch your work; we don't want to jeopardise things and cause a defensive reaction. We've spent many hours with people who have shown us friendship and kindness. But here we also are confronted, upset, knowing that things aren't right. What do we do with these thoughts and feelings? How can they be used helpfully to support a different way of working? In this chapter, we reflect on these questions to help you to navigate the complex terrain of encountering, processing and sharing 'bad practice'. We start by focusing on the challenges of feedback and defensiveness before presenting examples of 'bad practice' from our own research and illustrations of how we addressed these.

What's the problem with feedback?

When you start to change a system, there's a tacit agreement that things aren't perfect, just as when someone signs up to a course of psychotherapy it's with a realisation that something needs change. When an organisation invites an outsider in, there is a similar understanding: that you will become vulnerable to their critical gaze and that things will come up and will need to be dealt with. Contextual Safeguarding system change starts from the realisation that the current system isn't working for children harmed beyond their homes. This isn't a minor misalignment where a few children aren't getting quite the right response. We are talking about children at risk of death being treated as perpetrators or victims of sexual assault being left with no support. Fortunately, this is now a widely recognised problem: in 2018, when we invited social care departments to be part of the Scale-Up programme, 50 areas applied for the three places available.

There is a difference, however, between knowing there is a problem and finding a solution. Signing up for therapy can be a big step, but it doesn't lead to instant enlightenment. Organisations, like individuals, are complex and contradictory. There may be conflicting levels of acquiescence and openness to the need for change and the process for getting there. An organisation or team is a group, and in all groups people occupy different positions, often played out according to their roles (Owens 2015). The director may have invited you in, keen to hear your critical reflections, but the senior leaders may be less convinced, while practitioners may think it'll bring yet more scrutiny. We need to be sensitive to this and mindful that as we go in to observe and ask questions, those we are observing and questioning will be full of imaginings about what we're doing and thinking (Bondi 2003). They might be keen for us to see that while the *system* isn't working, they are personally doing everything they can. With such a complex set of emotions going on, offering feedback takes considerable skill and sensitivity.

Minimising defensiveness

Imagine you are a researcher who has worked through the tools described in Part I. You've paid close attention to the system you're working within and come up with some ideas for its improvement, some of which involve implied criticism of the professionals you have been observing and interviewing. To your dismay, your bright ideas are not so welcome among those who have worked in the system much longer than you. You don't understand 'how things are here', they say. It can be frustrating and embarrassing to try to deliver feedback that you feel is strongly evidenced and important only to have it batted away and ignored. But we need to accept that defensiveness is an extremely normal response when people feel vulnerable and scrutinised. Our role is to think carefully about how feedback is delivered and the environment in which it is received as well as the validity of what we want to say. Before sharing anything, draw on your team to sense check the appropriateness of what you want to say. You might have started to question if what you saw was '*that* bad' and if the feedback is needed at all. In this case, your team can help you see that it is our role to support professionals to reflect on how practice that has become normalised could actually be harmful. An example of this is described in Chapter 3, when it had become normal for children who had been stabbed or had stabbed another child to receive 'no further action' decisions because the harm was not attributable to parenting, despite these clearly reaching the statutory threshold for significant harm.

To minimise defensiveness, we must try to create the conditions where feedback can be heard and so that those you are giving feedback to are ready to hear and act on it. This process should start before the project begins. In Scale-Up, we had the luxury of choosing the sites we worked with. While this is unusual, there are nevertheless some activities that could help you during project set-up. Being clear about what the research involves and making sure that there is good buy-in from senior colleagues helped with our set-up. Because of the importance of partnership work in Contextual Safeguarding, we also made sure that senior leaders from related agencies, including the police, community safety and education, were on board. Of course, as we've said, senior buy-in does not mean that all practitioners will be enamoured with the idea of change. Because of this, it's a good idea to speak to and engage with practitioners to get a sense of their views and the challenges that might arise before beginning the work.

Once work is underway, a good strategy for managing the tension and minimising the defensiveness that could be generated by the presence of an external observer is to focus on the things that are going well – certainly at the beginning – and then gradually work on generating a shared view of what needs to change. As we explored in Chapter 6, the SPOC and other local leaders have a vital role in embedding cultural and systemic change. The researcher and the SPOC can create an allyship, a bond of trust that says: 'We understand things need to change.

We are in this together.' This reduces the sense of there being two sides: the critic and the receiver of criticism.

Taking the embedded approach described in this book is a very rich and rewarding way of working. But it's not always an easy path. It involves getting stuck in with the dynamics of an organisation and often becoming part of the messiness. One of the best ways to do this is to 'do the work' and play an active role in making changes. For example, at the very early stages of Contextual Safeguarding, we worked with one social worker in a site to create new 'context assessment triangles' (to facilitate assessments) and went back and forth on ideas of what could be included. We (the researchers and social worker) then took this to the rest of the social work team for feedback. In this instance, working alongside each other meant that we too were made vulnerable to the critical eye of other practitioners. We were not placing ourselves in the role of an expert who only ever delivers feedback and never receives it. And, trust us, deliver feedback they did!

Another important way to ensure feedback is received well is to be sensitive to how our feedback might be received. We need to be aware of under-the-surface activity – the culture of a place – and be mindful that our words can carry more weight than we might realise. As discussed in Chapter 4, we might be asked to reassure, give comment or feedback which feels very loaded and catches us off guard. For us, this happened quite a lot, as we were presented with work (for example, a policy document or practice tool) and asked for direct feedback, often as a practitioner was standing there. In these times, we would often rapidly ask ourselves: Is this their work? Are they looking for reassurance? Or actual advice? Working in this environment can be difficult, and you might find yourself feeling particularly self-conscious about occupying this space. We have certainly experienced worries about the sense of expectation people have for us and our work, as well as feeling people's frustration and even hostility about us scrutinising their work. It is not unusual to find yourself with a running commentary going on in your mind about how you are being perceived, and it is likely also the same for the workers who are being observed. An example of this is discussed by Jenny following a system review:

RESEARCHER REFLECTION

In the final system review of one site, I had to present findings from research around the pilot. This involved reading multiple case files. During this process I had been deeply upset by what I had found: the language used to discuss young people, the high number of cases that had been closed despite significant harm, and an apparent disdain for young people and general distrust of families that appeared to permeate the words and actions taken by professionals. This was exacerbated by the fact that this system review was taking place after we had been working together for three years; yet little seemed to have changed. As part of the review, I included quotes from the case files. For example, a case that was closed included the following: 'Although [young person] has suffered significant harm as he was a victim of a shooting he has made a full recovery and is not raising any concerns for his emotional or physical wellbeing.' Another noted: '[mum] has developed excellent skills in deflecting and rejecting support and assistance from professionals'.

The meeting took place online and I was leading it joined by many professionals from the site I personally really liked. I felt very caught in between. On the one hand I felt upset to think that a child who had been shot might not be seen as in need of support. But on the other hand, my doubts crept in: 'Is it really that bad?' Am I just naive because I'm not a social worker?' There was certainly always a dominant narrative in this site that they experienced some of the worst forms of harm and that the professionals here were hardened to working in situations of entrenched organised crime. I was conscious of my southern English accent in contrast to this area: How could I understand what it was like to work there? I felt bad at having to deliver negative feedback to hard-working professionals. I doubted my method and if I had got it right. But, once I had delivered the feedback, followed by a few moments of awkward silence, one professional spoke up. She said 'That was really hard. I could really see Jen that you found that hard to tell us. But thank you.' There was something about the way she said 'Jen' that really struck me. I could feel that although it was hard for both of us, the relationships we had established meant that not only did they trust what I said, they trusted the intention in why I had to deliver it. The rest of the meeting focused on how we could work together to make changes.

As you can see from this extract, this is hard, emotionally draining work, and it is important to acknowledge and give space to this. Giving difficult feedback was improved by several factors: the relationships we had established in sites; the support we had from the principal investigator to sense check findings; the reflective sessions where we rehearsed the presentation before and reflected on it after; and methods which allowed us to evidence things that felt intensely emotional. Even with an embedded approach to system change that is, arguably, more grounded in the principles of reciprocity, we can find ourselves encountering unexpected and often uncomfortable things. If we have developed trusting relationships, we can navigate these choppy waters and achieve some equally unexpected outcomes, but first we may need to grapple with some of the more problematic aspects of practice. How we process these things and how we share them with those involved are among the most significant parts of embedded research for system change.

'Bad practice'

What do we mean by 'bad practice'? We mean practice that troubles us because it is ethically challenging or upsetting. The result of our using the methods outlined in Part I is that we had become embedded and enmeshed in how children's social care operated in sites and the cultures in place there. This work was often very rewarding when we were directly able to enact change we felt would improve experiences for young people and families. Yet, of course, our very being there suggested things needed to change. And often our methods led us to unearthing practice that caused us concern. The overall aim of our research was to understand how the system could address extra-familial harm. However, because our work was underpinned by Contextual Safeguarding, we also needed any changes we helped bring about to engage not only with the basic principles of that (the four domains – see Chapter 1) but also the values that underpin it. This meant that as we were becoming 'embedded' in sites, we needed to ensure that our work was committed to being 'strengths based', 'rights based', 'ecological', 'collaborative', rooted in the reality of young people and families' lives, as well as hopeful and alive to structural harm. So, what did we do when faced with evidence that practice was not contextual and also ran counter to these values? Before discussing *how* we delivered that feedback, we present several short and modified examples of practice that we felt opposed the values and domains of Contextual Safeguarding. We have drawn these examples from Scale-Up and also the last eight years of doing embedded research. They are deliberatively abstracted and modified for anonymity because we feel a loyalty to the people that we work with. It is not our intention to name and shame, and we don't want people to be preoccupied with trying to figure out which site did what.

EXAMPLE 1
MEETING OBSERVATION

While observing a meeting for a pilot, we observed the senior social worker inform professionals that any information provided by young people should be fed into a police website.

EXAMPLE 2
MEETING OBSERVATION

In a panel meeting, professionals around the table collectively cheered when they realised a young person would soon be turning 18 and they would no longer be required to offer them support.

EXAMPLE 3
MEETING OBSERVATION

One site used a rating system to define the risk posed to young people. When a professional asked why one young person had scored 109, the chair replied: 'You get 10 points for suicide or attempted suicide and there were some incidents while he was "inside."'

Giving feedback on 'bad practice'

EXAMPLE 4
DOCUMENT REVIEW
A meeting to discuss harm and exploitation to young people [was] referred to as the 'risky behaviours panel'.

EXAMPLE 5
CASE FILE REVIEW
A 14-year-old girl that was tricked into going to a park and was the victim of a group sexual assault [was] described as 'putting herself at risk'.

EXAMPLE 6
CONVERSATION WITH A PROFESSIONAL
A professional that we had worked with for several years suggest[ed] an intervention with young people at risk of exploitation and abuse, that involved taking them to visit a youth offending institution to 'experience what it was like' to deter them from wanting to go there.

EXAMPLE 7
MEETING OBSERVATION
[In a] meeting ... increasing CCTV and surveillance of young people were described as positive 'Contextual Safeguarding' interventions.

All these examples made us feel something. They frustrated us, upset us and even annoyed us. Sometimes, these feeling were not immediately obvious, and it wasn't until we reflected with others that we saw that practice was not right. Many times, however, it was clear that practice was harmful, but we were in contexts – for example, physically sitting in a meeting – that made it difficult to immediately process our feelings. Depending on your professional background, these examples might seem shocking or they might feel fairly mundane and business as usual. Some of the feelings we had about these examples relate directly to the values of Contextual Safeguarding. So if you are reading Examples 1 and 7 and aren't quite sure what the fuss is about, it may be helpful to read our other research in this area (Wroe and Lloyd 2020; Owens and Lloyd 2023). For us, we found it very challenging to manage our feelings. We wondered how we could provide feedback and constructive criticism, especially in those times when we were upset and even angry at what we found.

Feeling the feelings

Before preparing to give feedback, it is important to manage the feelings that you have had in response to what you have seen. If you are feeling moved, upset or angry, it's probably not the time to give feedback. However, there is no shortcut to getting from a place of awful feelings of horror and pain to a place of understanding and learning. For us, hearing about or seeing practice that is out of kilter with our ethics and values is often upsetting. We are not saying that we are always correct and that our morals and ethics are always perfectly aligned, but rather that we need to acknowledge that as researchers and external agents coming into a team, we have a unique perspective, and the more we can align this with the experiences of young people and families, the more useful these feelings can be for bringing about change. It is an opportunity to see things in a multi-perspectival way, if we allow it, which can lead to a very rich and rewarding way of helping a system grow – but it is not easy.

The first thing we do is talk about it with someone in the research team. In Example 6, the researcher talked to our team about how frustrating and upsetting it was to have been working for so long with someone and for them to still suggest things that seem to be so against Contextual Safeguarding values like the idea that a way to help create safety for young people is to make prison seem less appealing to them, as if they are choosing to be harmed in order to go to prison. The way we managed our feelings about these types of things was always having someone we could contact and call after an activity had taken place that might be distressing. We ensured that someone else from the team was available to talk following activities such as case review, meeting observation or engagement with young people and families. And we had additional space to discuss these feelings in our reflective meetings.

The next thing to say is that we do not stay in the place of anger, disappointment and shock. There is a real danger if we do this that we will simply replicate a 'them and us' binary. We could use this information if we wanted to make ourselves feel smug and take our own moral high ground. On the other hand, we could come out raging, insisting that all social work practice and welfare services are entirely problematic. These are both tempting positions to take. At times, we are certainly guilty of occupying each of these as we navigated our way around this complex work, and it's likely that you will too. However, the method that we have developed involves working *with* problematic practice to support learning and growth.

Giving feedback and channelling feelings

We did not give feedback for every single piece of 'bad practice' we witnessed. This type of nitpicking would very likely break down any relationships we had and remove the possibility that change would be made. We tried mostly to 'see the bigger picture'. Broadly speaking, there were two ways we acted on practice that was problematic or troubling. First, where we felt it was important for sites to be aware and learn from practice, we fed it back to them to help them make changes. Second, we channelled our feelings and learning into broader resources, including training, policy, presentations – where the impact may be felt at a larger scale. There were several ways we fed back to sites: at system reviews; to the SPOC; or directly to individual practitioners. It is worth noting, though, that unless we felt there had been a significant safeguarding issue, we did not provide feedback about individual practitioners. Instead, our feedback focused on general themes and trends, illustrated by examples. This is because much of the 'bad practice' we saw was born out of an environment, organisation culture and system that had normalised it. And we focused initially on the more promising activities we had seen. Our approach to delivering feedback was informed by taking a restorative approach, illustrated through the social discipline window.

The social discipline window

The social discipline window (Wachtel 1999; Figure 7.1) is a concept that describes four basic approaches to maintaining social norms and behavioural boundaries, represented as different

Figure 7.1: The social discipline window

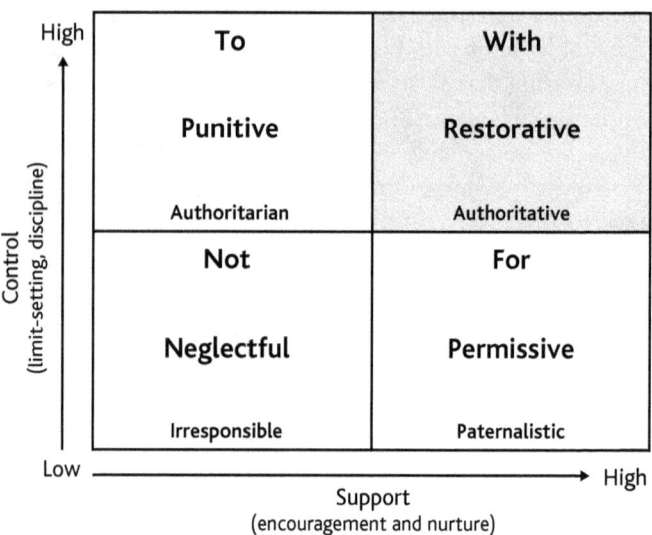

Source: Wachtel (1999)

combinations of high or low control and high or low support. In this framework, 'control' refers to limit-setting and discipline, and 'support' includes encouragement and nurturing.

The restorative domain (highlighted in grey) combines both high control and high support and is characterised by doing things *with* people rather than *to* them or *for* them. The fundamental unifying hypothesis of restorative practices is that 'human beings are happier, more cooperative and productive, and more likely to make positive changes in their behaviour when those in positions of authority do things with them, rather than to them or for them' (Wachtel and McCold 2004, para 2). This hypothesis maintains that the punitive and authoritarian *to* mode and the permissive and paternalistic *for* mode are not as effective as the restorative *with* mode, which is participatory and engaging (Braithwaite 1989).

This is a helpful concept to support us in thinking about our positionality and relationship to the systems we are researching. We aim in our methods to move closer to working 'with' our research partners. When we're working in children's services, however, our partners are various and do not always agree or see things in the same way. The social worker context – the rules at play that dictate, shape and limit what type of social work is possible – is not the same as young people's context, which is not always the same as their parents and carers' context. The people who live in communities and those who run businesses where young people spend time also have their own experience and perspectives. It is our role to stand in the centre of these perspectives, with an awareness of power – particularly in relation to the marginalisation of young people and the task of increasing their sense of safety in communities – to make sense of what needs to change. The best way we know of doing this is to try to follow restorative principles and to find an appropriate form of authority. There is always the danger of giving up by either neglectful or permissive responses, and there is also the temptation to become punitive by telling people what to do, trying to control them. But, as the window shows, the way to achieve the best possible outcomes is to provide a high level of support, encouragement and nurturing, along with high levels of control (Figure 7.1).

To apply this in relation to feedback and system change means holding in balance things that are often contrasting. The key message of this book is that if you want to make real-life change in children's social care, you need to do it with an appreciation of both *structure* and *relationships*. Understanding control as 'boundaries and discipline' doesn't mean acting punitively, but creating appropriate limits to, and expectations of, the work and being held accountable. We did not give upsetting feedback 'off the cuff', nor did we hold on to evidence of problematic practice through fear of upsetting. We created appropriate spaces and times where feedback was prepared for and support was in place. Of course, there will always be the fear that what we say might undermine a relationship, but we are supported by a continued need to position ourselves at the heart of communities and to think about what young people (those often absent from the room) need to live safer lives. We turn now to some of the specific ways we provided feedback.

Giving feedback to individuals

The formal route for delivering feedback was through system reviews. However, in this meeting, rarely is it suitable or practical to go through every individual challenge that has arisen. Furthermore, we often did not want professionals to be caught off guard, feeling they hadn't had some warning about what was about to come before the 'big reveal' in a formal meeting.

Several of the examples listed previously were managed individually with professionals. Example 1, where a senior social worker suggested feeding information from young people to a police website, felt particularly sensitive. This is because the person who had said this was also the SPOC, so we were directly feeding back to them that the approach *they* had taken contravened the values and principles of Contextual Safeguarding. This was not easy feedback to give and their response was, possibly predictably, defensive. They reminded us about police protocols and the unique cultural challenges they were facing due to working in an area of high deprivation and organised crime. Rather than labour the point, we raised the issue again at the system review once we'd had time to discuss the issue more with colleagues and present further reasons why informing the police of issues young people raise may undermine relationships. In this meeting, it was clear that this challenge landed with some professionals and not others. At this point, we felt there was little more we could do. However, coincidentally, a few months later this site attended a national workshop we held with other professionals where we discussed approaches that built trust with young people or increased surveillance (Wroe and Lloyd 2020). This was an environment where they were not being given direct feedback on their own work but joined in listening to others critique punitive approaches. It was only after *this* workshop where they had engaged in a more theoretical discussion about practice, and perhaps didn't feel so personally confronted, that change started to happen. This site asked for an individual meeting with us after the workshop and then started delivering their own workshops to try and shift approaches to build trust with young people. This was a change we would never have foreseen in the initial meeting with the SPOC.

A similar thing happened in relation to Example 7, where CCTV and surveillance of young people were put forward as positive Contextual Safeguarding practices. Following this meeting, the researcher observing the meeting was asked to stay on the call. The chair of the meeting, someone the researcher liked and respected, asked for her feedback on what she had seen. From the demeanour of the chair, it was clear that they were looking for praise for the approach. Unfortunately, this was not something the researcher felt able to give. They were stuck. It didn't feel the right time to give feedback, especially when it appeared the opposite of what the chair might be expecting or wanting to hear. But it would feel disingenuous and potentially damaging if they lied. In this instance, the researcher discussed elements of the meeting that were good before discussing how increased CCTV and surveillance may not align with the welfare intentions of the meeting. The chair responded in defence and reiterated what the law said (we have found that people often retreat to the law and crime prevention in defensiveness). This was a hard position to navigate, because we are dealing with our own feelings of imposter syndrome and concerns about not knowing enough. Although there was little more discussion, at a later point, the chair told us that she had learnt so much from the project and was grateful. We have no way of knowing if that was related to incidents like this one – we can only hope.

Feedback in system reviews

In many ways, we found providing individual feedback challenging. In these encounters we were often required to provide robust defences for our emerging soft-sounding 'feelings' and 'values' before we'd had the chance to reflect with our research colleagues and get our message straight. But the candid and conversational nature of this way of giving feedback likely contributed to their usefulness to sites. In system reviews, however, we were supported with a team of researchers, including the principal investigator of the programme. Likewise, professionals in sites were supported by their colleagues and could assume that any challenges raised were not about them personally but about the organisation.

In Chapter 4, we outlined the approach we took to system reviews. This involved a range of analysis sessions focused on the data from a site, preparing the presentation and slides and rehearsing our feedback with the principal investigator. All of this laid the groundwork to ensure a rigorous approach to data collection and analysis and that the feedback was appropriate, and it prepared us for potential questions or challenges. It is worth noting that most system reviews were positive; there were only a few instances when the feedback felt particularly stark. What we found was important for these meetings was the (perceived) rigour of data – particularly direct quotes or evidence – coupled with a caring and relational foundation to the delivery of feedback. This was evidenced previously in the example of the system review that involved delivering feedback where a boy had been shot (see the 'Minimising defensiveness' section). In instances where we felt upset or angered by what the research had revealed, there was a delicate balance between feeling a responsibility to the young people impacted by the system and feeling a responsibility to the professionals in the site. This is a hard space to navigate on your own, and it's important that findings and feelings have a place to be processed before feeding back.

Channelling feelings

As mentioned, it was not appropriate or feasible to feed back every individual piece of 'bad practice' we witnessed or everything that we heard that moved or upset us. But even if we did not feed something back, it still informed our work. Example 2 (where the professionals were pleased they wouldn't have to offer support to a young person after their 18th birthday) and Example 3 (where a young person's suicide attempts were discussed) were not fed back directly to sites but were used more broadly to illustrate the culture of organisations, and we have since used these examples to develop training resources for professionals nationally (with consent from the sites). We made example training videos based on anonymised versions of these vignettes and used them with young people and professionals to highlight problematic practice and build support to make changes. You might really, really want to tell someone something was bad and be overtaken by an emotional response, but it is important to navigate when and how this should be done. Just because something isn't used in a system review doesn't mean it can't be used to make changes on a wider level. Think and develop effective avenues for challenging your feelings through reflective sessions, and then use this evidence to build outputs and resources that make an impact and change. Although it doesn't take away from the upset and horror of what happened to the young person or parent involved, we can at least feel grateful to be part of a process where what happened to them can hopefully be turned into change at a larger level.

Contextualising 'bad practice'

In Contextual Safeguarding, we evidently are keen on context. We believe that young people's experiences and behaviour happen within a context rather than in isolation. We draw on Bourdieu (1984) to think about the 'rules at play' in a particular social context and think about how we can alter these to give young people different experiences that are safe, with more choices. For example, if a child is carrying a knife, rather than seeing this as the result of them being a 'bad' individual, Contextual Safeguarding, drawing on Bourdieu, allows us to think more about what the context must be like that results in a child feeling the need to carry a knife. Not only do we apply this thinking to our work on extra-familial harm, but we use this as a philosophical stance that we bring to system change work. In Scale-Up, once we had reflected, cried and bemoaned the problematic practices that we saw, we started to apply some of the same theoretical concepts to our wider system change work. We thought about the contrast in language used in different areas and then asked questions about the contexts in which this was taking place: What were the local cultures or rules at play in each area? Why did professionals feel the need to 'carry' problematic language and practice with them? What were they defending against? Was this the same everywhere, and if not, what opportunities did practitioners have to think and act differently?

We were fortunate that by working in several sites we could draw on evidence that allowed us to show different ways of working. By looking at examples of 'bad practice', we supported each other to consider the underlying structures, systems and cultures that may lead to different ways of working. For example, we could see overly punitive police-led responses as underpinned, in some instances, by a fear of getting too relationally close to young people at risk of death. We hypothesised that in contexts where practitioners lacked containment (good supervision, management and resources), coming close to young people in such risky situations could feel overwhelming. This often resulted in overly bureaucratic risk management processes (Lloyd, Hickle et al 2023). Cheering when a child turns 18 we understood to be part of a wider system problem of a lack of effective resources, misalignment with adult services and gaps in support for chairs in meetings to set the appropriate tone and intent. Working with examples across several sites led us to explore what might be going on culturally in a site where there were many examples of problematic language. This doesn't mean 'letting people off the hook'. Children's social care is not a benign system. Even if individuals within it have the right motivation, the wider context is one of sexism, classism and racial inequality that is baked into the system historically (Roberts 2021; Hunter and Wroe 2022). It is important not only to understand the culture of a place but also to consider the historical, political and economic drivers that create these circumstances, and we see it as our role to very much advocate for changes to these at a national policy scale (Firmin and Lloyd 2022).

But if you are faced with 'bad practice', rather than jumping first to this more philosophical position, we urge you to first *feel your feelings*. Shout, moan, cry. Speak with others. When the dust has settled, support one another to ask questions about the culture, history, policies or organisation that created this context. Use this as your ammunition to make plans for change.

Conclusion

Taking a relational approach to changing children's social care is both costly and demanding, but also rich and rewarding when we seek to develop the 'human' aspect of human services. This requires acknowledging the boundaries of your role. It is not your role to point out every problem you see, nor is it beneficial to ignore 'bad practice' due to fear of upsetting a relationship. It's important to maintain an 'independent' stance, but this doesn't mean retreating to being an 'objective' and 'passive' observer. In using the tools outlined in Part I, we can anchor ourselves to an evidence base that will support us to shift attitudes and unearth harmful practices and cultures, many of which may have gone unnoticed and have become normalised by those in the system. The learning from Part II is that this evidence, combined with relationships, can help us create the foundations for real-life change. Remember that there is a reason why you have been invited in: something isn't right. We close with some key pointers:

1. It is important to consider the range of ways that feedback will be delivered and plan for more formal opportunities through system reviews.
2. Consider and plan for ways to minimise defensive responses to feedback. Ensure sites are engaged and want to be part of a change process.
3. Ensure you have regular opportunities to reflect on practice, particularly around activities that may be upsetting or triggering.
4. Feel your feelings. Feel angry and upset; don't jump too quickly to trying to find explanations.
5. Then take time to contextualise your findings by asking questions about the culture, history, policies and structure of a place.
6. Try not to take a superior stance, but one of humility and care.

PART III

Theories and learning from doing system change in children's social care

In the following haikus, we muse on the ideas of system change and the role of theory to illuminate this. A haiku is a three-line poem where the first line consists of five syllables, the second of seven syllables and the third of five syllables. The beauty of a haiku is that it condenses an idea, so writing one really makes you focus in on the essence of what it is you want to say. You can play with writing your own haikus from your research and practice.

Hope
You went and did it
So it's not just a theory
Worlds can be safer

Invitation
She gently said no
Let's try a different way
Will you come with us?

Figure 9.1
Circles in circles
Connecting inside outside
Whole holding space

Splitting
Move from 'You' to 'We'
In messy complexity
The blame dissipates

8

Reasons to be hopeful

Introduction

The research that forms the basis of this book was undertaken at a time of global change. In 2020, one year into the project, much of the world went into lockdown as nations tried to battle the spreading COVID-19 virus. Since then, we have been faced with continuing national and global challenges: political instability; austerity; war; rising costs; and cuts to services. In the UK, these changes are set against a backdrop of hostility, particularly to those people most in need, growing demands to strengthen national borders (Parker et al 2022), emotionally charged cultural wars and divisive politics (Duffy et al 2021) and the promotion of punitive and sanctions-based responses to harm (Case and Bateman 2020). When children cause harm, the news is dominated with petitions to remove their protections afforded through anonymity (BBC 2024), as though justice can only be served by publicly shaming a few individual young people. Rarely do we hear about the need for compassion or community in addressing youth violence and harm. The public – apparently – wants tougher sanctions, longer sentences and a justice system for children that looks and sounds like the one we have for adults. If you, like us, see the world differently, is there much to be hopeful for? What is the point of doing system change if the systems around us are resistant to change? The first two parts of this book have been very close to practice and very much about the doing of system change work. In this final part, we take a small step back to reflect on what we have learnt about systems change from a slightly different vantage point. From this perspective, Part III considers how we can recognise and value real-life system change. When it comes to the end of your project, what will you have achieved and how will you know that? We share some stories to explore what we've learnt about this quite difficult process. Then we look at the theoretical frameworks that have helped underpin our work, considering how they have been integral to the conversations and decisions we've made.

In the conclusion to the second book on Contextual Safeguarding, Carlene Firmin writes: 'I encourage you to come to the end of this book as I do – on the side of hope' (2020, p 256). At that time, she believed that there was much to be hopeful for in the development of Contextual Safeguarding. It had moved from merely a framework, theory or idea to real change. She showed us how the solutions to the seemingly unsolvable problem of addressing extra-familial harm had been created with, and alongside, practitioners. These changes were emerging through shifts in the systems and cultures of children's social care, showing us that when children are harmed beyond their front door, there is something we can do about it. We too want to end this book on a hopeful message. We want to show you that real-life change is possible.

In this chapter, we share with you some examples from our own work of building system change in children's social care. Whether you are interested in Contextual Safeguarding system change specifically or work in a field far removed from adolescent safeguarding, we believe that hope is a vital part of a system change method that requires so much of us emotionally and relationally. We focus on examples of how the approach outlined in Parts I and II contributed to system changes that improved responses to extra-familial harm. Because of the wider audience of this book, beyond just those interested in adolescent safeguarding, rather than focusing on how extra-familial harm was reduced (you can find an example of this in Owens 2023), we consider more generally how embedded methods helped to bring about changes to systems.

Throughout this book, we have been emphasising the role of relationships in system change. In writing this book, we entered into another relationship, one we haven't yet mentioned – our relationship with you, our reader. As we share examples of system change and the impacts we have contributed to, we feel nervous of jeopardising our relationship with you by coming across as if we are 'boasting'. We feel inherently uncomfortable about claiming successes are due, even in part, to our efforts, and as women we are socialised into modesty. At the same time, we are proud of the work we have done in partnership with our colleagues in sites so it's with this ambivalence that we share these stories of hope with you.

Incremental change

Let's begin by situating the 'impact' of our work within the current neoliberal organisational context. When we're doing system change, and especially at the point when we have to talk about it to funders and commissioners, it's very easy to fall into the language of 'transformation' (Lefevre et al 2024). After all, who wants to give large amounts of money to projects that offer 'slow and steady incremental change over decades'? But this is exactly the sort of change we need to be working towards and celebrating. For us, being hopeful is not about promising unrealistic, unachievable things. It's not some 'pie in the sky' idea of creating a perfect world, nor is it about telling a good story to make things sound more impressive than they really are. It is about believing that change can happen, that systems and cultures can shift, but knowing that it won't be overnight and might look, at first at least, quite modest. But small shifts are so important. It is the incremental, marginal gains that are not only achievable (Factor and Ackerley 2019) but over time will have the best chance of being sustained and affecting bigger shifts. So, we can do away with neoliberal notions of large-scale impact and transformation and embrace instead something closer to real life, which is, ultimately, the only sort of change that is within our reach.

In Chapter 9, we explore our theoretical grounding, which draws on, among other things, critical realist ideas about the possibility of emancipatory change and is reinforced by our experiences of creating system change. Throughout this book, we have described how children's social care and related safeguarding systems are far from benign. It's not just a case of changing a few processes, pivoting what we used to do for familial harm to extra-familial harm. Young people facing exploitation and abuse have this harm compounded by safeguarding services, where there can be a culture of racism, sexism, adultification and individual blame, reinforcing colonial, misogynistic ideology (Bernard and Harris 2016). So, you might be thinking, why should we even try to reform these systems? Shouldn't we just scrap it all and start again? We understand these arguments and have a lot of sympathy for them. But we have come to the position that despite how alluring the promise of abolition may be, particularly when faced with the pain and anger of harmful systems, we are hopeful pragmatists. We have decided to focus our efforts on imagining change from within the current system rather than calling for it to be abolished entirely.

We believe that the most realistic way to change systems is to harness the influence and efforts of professionals who help to make up the system by working day to day within it. It's not that we don't sometimes wish another, more radical path was possible. But over time and through many discussions, we return to the need to work with what we have, and we see this as the most realistic way to make change. To abolish the current system and replace it with something else would require a political long-term vision and corresponding financial investment that we find hard to imagine in this current moment. When we talk about working with professionals within systems to create change, we do so with a note of caution, however. We've learnt that when a small number of people (say, practitioners, managers and researchers) are tasked on behalf of an organisation to change systems that are beset with complex structural and systemic issues, it can lead to individuals feeling demoralised under a heavy individual burden for delivering something that is often beyond their reach (Lefevre et al 2024). We've seen how professionals can have very high expectations of themselves, giving a great deal and paying a high personal price. If the hoped for change is not forthcoming, they can feel guilty and imagine that its due to some deficiency within their work. So while we say that change is possible, we also want to emphasise that it's not the responsibility of individuals alone to tackle engrained systemic, cultural and structural issues. Contextual Safeguarding is all about moving *away* from notions of individualised responsibility to collective and community-based change, and this is how we also approach system change.

The work we have done in Contextual Safeguarding has, on many accounts, been unprecedented and grand. From Carlene Firmin's PhD thesis in 2015, it was took just three years for the concept of Contextual Safeguarding to enter into statutory safeguarding policy through its inclusion into *Working Together to Safeguard Children* (HM Government 2018). In less than a decade, children's services in over 80 local authorities have committed to implementing the approach, and a network has been formed of thousands of professionals dedicated to its cause. At the practice level, in partnership with professionals we've created a new safeguarding pathway for children facing harm outside the home (Firmin 2024), new interventions to change contexts and new meetings where groups and places, rather than individual young people, are discussed (Contextual Safeguarding 2022b). But the radical ideas that underlie Contextual Safeguarding have been much slower to take hold. Shifting the system culture has been, and continues to be, slow and difficult. Despite our best efforts, we still see a preoccupation with individual behaviour rather than social conditions (Owens and Lloyd 2023), with sanctions rather than welfare (Lloyd, Manister et al 2023) and surveillance and monitoring rather than participation and support (Wroe and Manister 2024). But, despite this, all is not lost. There are glimmers of hope. Change is happening in ways that we could never have planned for or foreseen. This is less about the dramatic lightbulb moments and more about glittering gems that show us that real-life change is possible. When we look beyond ideals of transformation and focus on incremental change, then exciting things can start to happen.

Stories of system and culture change

The following stories are taken from examples of Contextual Safeguarding system change work within children's social care departments, in partnership with other agencies. At the end of the Scale-Up project, we produced an online toolkit to support others in their implementation of Contextual Safeguarding practice (Contextual Safeguarding 2022b). Within this toolkit, is a catalogue of responses (or interventions) that we collected during the project, presented as one-page entries, to inspire others to try similar approaches. The stories below are based on examples in this catalogue, with some details changed for anonymity. For each example, we have tried to trace how the approaches described in Parts I and II of this book led to real-life system change.

Physical safety in a location

In Part II, we explored the importance of relationships to system change and the importance of relationships for creating and changing a system's culture. We talked about how culture underpins and influences the rate and extent of change that is possible, so much so that as we use the tools and methods to map and understand systems and make system change plans, we must consider how these changes are enabled, or not, by the dominant culture of a system. In the Scale-Up project, some sites worked explicitly to harness or change their culture, and this was a large factor in enabling their system change plan. For others, working on culture was much more challenging. In these places, changes still took place but the lack of engagement with culture impacted the results, meaning that the outcome of the changes did not always align to the Contextual Safeguarding framework and values. Conversely, in places where there were small shifts, this had a large impact on what happened there. This was particularly the case in one site.

The people in this site were extremely friendly and positive towards us, but it felt like our methods didn't quite work for them. Especially at the start, we felt ourselves to be overly academic, perhaps a bit out of touch with their reality. We had a research plan and tools we wanted to use. We asked them for lists of meetings to observe and written documents to analyse. These requests seemed to be in contrast to the more fluid and organic style and culture of the site. At times, we felt like we were just running behind them, not knowing something was happening until it has finished. It just didn't work for them to give us lots of advance notice of events so we could plan them into our busy schedules. On more than one occasion, we were met by bemused professionals who had forgotten we were coming. But, over time, the relationship changed. A member of the research team started to work more closely with two or three professionals from the site, and it was through these stronger relationships that a way to work together emerged:

> RESEARCHER REFLECTION
>
> I suppose it started with getting together for regular meetings, probably most weeks, to plan a pilot. Rather than setting out to do a new piece of work, we agreed that the pilot would actually be a review of four context-based interventions, looking at the extent to which these aligned with their new policy document that set out their thresholds for responding to extra-familial harm for individuals and context. This was about finding our place in this system where so much change had taken place and seeing how we could support them to consolidate this into a pathway and process that could be followed by the growing team of workers and partners, beyond just the SPOC. It was very much about finding how our roles could work together and now it felt like this finally clicked. Meeting online every week helped to break down any idea of us being the university 'flying in'. It felt like we were much more side by side. On a practical note, we created a table to look at the four interventions, with a consistent set of questions to ask about each one. The SPOC talked through each one and we recorded the conversations and she pointed me to other people to speak to. In between the meetings she also populated the table with links to other documents so I built up a rich picture of what they were doing. This loose structure gave us something to work on together but in between talking about the pilot, the SPOC would be always telling me about new things she was doing or thinking about doing. As these were more 'live', there was more chance for us to shape them together. It felt like through the structure of the weekly meetings and pilot, we also found a way to move beyond retrospective work (where we heard about things quite a bit after the event) and to be more involve in the work as it was happening.

This site made significant changes to their system. For example, meetings that focused on individual children and young people were changed to have a broader focus on places and peer groups. The role of young people as partners increased significantly through the introduction of a young people's panel. The extra-familial harm 'team', which had been just one person when we arrived, increased to include a team of social workers working alongside youth workers. One of the greatest strengths of this site was the way they formed relationships with partners, but they were often limited in this through a more rigid and traditional framing of what social care focused on (that is, harm in families). By capitalising on the rich culture of working relationally this site already had, we were able to support them to make system change that influenced the way harm to adolescents was tackled.

Working with the Contextual Safeguarding team appeared to give this site a vision and mandate to use their existing strong relational and responsive culture for the purpose of creating safety in extra-familial contexts. They became so adept at working together that when an issue arose that was beyond the usual remit for children's social care, the partnership adapted quickly to support and lead the local community. This situation arose during a very hot summer. Local teenagers started swimming in rivers in the city and one got into trouble. When professionals heard about this, they realised that although it was not related to their usual work of looking at exploitation and violence, this issue could still be thought of as extra-familial harm. The partnership understood that it was their role to create a safe environment for young people, so this was very much within their remit. Having created pathways to tackle harm in communities (rather than just in families), they had established strong relationships and routes into creating physical safety for young people in this location. The partnership, under the leadership of social care, took a sensible approach to reducing the risks. They didn't spend ages wondering whose role it was to do things or whether they could or should erect barriers or CCTV around the area. Instead, they pulled in relevant partners to make a plan. One service went out and put up new buoyancy aids all around the river. The fire service agreed to regularly clear the river of obstructions, and the youth workers started to visit the areas and talk to young people about the risks of swimming there and how to keep safe. The group also put up signs with location information based on 'what3words' so that should anyone be in distress, they could quickly be found by the emergency services. The impact of this was much reduced risk of harm to young people and for the family of children who had got into trouble in the river, the sense that their children's experiences had helped to create safety for others.

School assessments to tackle harmful sexual behaviour

School context assessments are a method for assessing harm that might be happening in schools. They developed out of the first system change project the Contextual Safeguarding programme undertook with the London Borough of Hackney and subsequent research projects (Lloyd et al 2020; Contextual Safeguarding Network 2021). Traditionally, when harm happened between students in schools – for example, sexual harassment – the school would be unlikely to receive a safeguarding response (Lloyd 2019). In those that did, the students were often responded to individually – for example, each of the children involved would be referred and assessed separately. This type of response did not try to address the cultural and contextual nature of harm that was happening, such as a broader culture of sexism that created authorising and normalising environments for the harm to take place. However, the Contextual Safeguarding programme, in partnership with practitioners, have developed school context assessments intended to support safeguarding professionals to assess the cultural and systemic nature of harm happening in schools. These assessments draw on the methods outlined in Part I, including: the meeting observation method – through observations of school meetings; the embedded ethnographic method – through spending time in the school environment and going along to meetings and lessons; and the case review method – through reviews of safeguarding logs. These methods were incorporated into a specific assessment framework for schools (Contextual Safeguarding Network 2021) that formed the basis of the system change we were involved in with both schools and children's social care.

During the Scale-Up project, several sites used the school assessment method as part of their pilots (see Chapter 4). In one place, a team of social workers worked together with a school to use the method to respond to harmful sexual behaviour that was happening in the school. There had been incidents of sexual violence in the girls' toilets and non-consensual sharing of sexual imagery online. Using the assessment methods developed as part of the Contextual Safeguarding programme, the social workers ran exercises, such as reviewing school policies and running focus groups with parents and students, to understand the culture of the school. Following this assessment, the social work team held a 'school context conference', attended by school leadership, parents, education stakeholders and student representatives. Much like a child protection conference, the focus of the school context conference was on discussing harm that may be impacting the students and creating a plan for change. The conference led to agreement on goals, such as 'we want the girls' toilets to be safer', and creating a plan for change – for example, engaging a voluntary and community sector organisation to work with the school. The team planned a review conference three months later and carried out a survey to understand how safe students felt and find out if further incidents had occurred.

Changing the culture of how parents and young people are viewed and treated

We firmly believe that most social care professionals sign up to system change because they want to help and support people and not to judge them or restrict their rights. Even when we have witnessed exceptionally problematic practice, when we have heard of children being described as 'prostituting themselves' and parents being called 'liars', we believed that we were seeing people with good intentions, impacted by cultures and systems that have normalised harmful ways of thinking and acting. A fundamental aspect of our system change work has been naming and tackling these cultural harms. For example, in most of the sites we worked with, originally the preoccupation and focus of children's social care resulted in parents being responsibilised and blamed for harm happening to their children (Thornhill 2023). We also saw how when professionals held negative attitudes towards adolescents, this restricted the opportunities and responses available to them. However, by encouraging a rights-based partnership approach with parents and young people, we saw these cultures – and the systems – change.

In one site, a 13-year-old boy had been going missing and not attending school. Professionals were worried that he was spending time with people that sell drugs and that he might be being groomed to sell them too. His mum was very worried and wanted to move him away from the area – a solution that would have been extremely disruptive for the boy and his whole family. Normally when faced with an issue like this, it can be difficult for social workers to suggest many changes. Moving children away can often feel like the only unfortunate response possible when professionals feel they have little power to alter the exploitation occurring in the area (Firmin, Wroe et al 2022). However, in this site, they had – through the Scale-Up project – created a pathway to assess and respond to contexts. They were already working to tackle the exploitation that was happening, and which the boy was linked to. The social worker was able to comfort the boy's mum and talk about all the action that was happening to prevent the harm, sending the message that it wasn't the 'fault' of the parents and that others were there to help. The mum felt happier knowing what work was taking place and that the family would be supported to stay locally.

System change that tackles systemic and structural harm

Working in the context of harm and abuse against children is not easy. We wish we had a magic wand and could solve the problem of exploitation and violence against children, but no such thing exists. In Chapter 7, we look at the equally, if not more, upsetting reality of the harm that can occur from systems themselves. In many ways, although it is always upsetting to hear about, inter-personal harm (like exploitation and violence) is certainly not a surprise when we work in children's social care. But witnessing harm directly from the systems and structures designed to keep young people safe – in the name of safeguarding – can be the most painful thing to witness. It is for this reason that although our system change work often sets out with the intention of creating systems designed to respond to extra-familial harm, in reality much of our work becomes about tackling the systemic and structural causes of harms. This work can be particularly challenging. Perhaps most professionals are on board with the idea that their systems don't support them to address harm outside family homes, but turning the spotlight on themselves, on their own practice, this can be painful and hard to bear. We discussed how we navigate this in Chapter 7. Here we share a story about addressing systemic racism.

In one area, concerns were raised with social care about a group of teenagers who were coming to the attention of the police. The group was spending time in a local park and being approached by people known to sell drugs. Professionals were worried that the young people may be being exploited to sell drugs. The social workers, who had developed 'context assessments' as part of their Contextual Safeguarding system change work, decided they wanted to do some work with the group of young people. Traditionally, this might have included working with the group to highlight the risks of exploitation and partnering with the police to disrupt the exploitation. However, by using the assessment tools developed in their Contextual Safeguarding system change plan, they learnt about the broader contexts that may be impacting the situation. All the young people were from the same minoritised ethnic group and attended the same school. The social workers realised that the school disproportionately excluded children from this ethnic group. They felt that if the students were able to safely attend school, this could reduce the risks they faced in the community. A meeting was held between the school and social work team, arranged and chaired by independent Family Group Conference coordinators. The conversation was not easy. Staff discussed how a lack of common language and culture with these young people and their families had impacted how they'd engaged with them. They had turned a 'blind eye' to them; prejudice and discrimination were clearly part of the reasons why the young people were being excluded. In this sensitive conversation, the school staff were supported to see this and come up with solutions to tackle these issues.

The views held by the school were not isolated to them. Researchers in the team had also witnessed, during meeting observations, language that suggested racist attitudes about this ethnic group were held among staff in social care and other agencies. Alongside the work taking place in the school, conversations were being held between the site SPOC and the research team. The SPOC noticed that we (the research team) had included the word 'racism' on a slide that was due to be presented at an upcoming system review meeting the following week (for a description of system review meetings, see Chapter 4). We generally shared our slides with the SPOCs ahead of system review meetings to check in with them about any sensitive or 'political' issues. We had a good relationship with this SPOC and there was a strong sense of trust between us, but she told the researcher leading the pilot that she was nervous and worried that the word 'racism' would reflect badly on the site and have larger implications – for example, it might be seen by the social care inspectorate, Ofsted. This was not a likely outcome, as these findings would not be shared with the inspectorate (or any other partner), but it was clear there was a lot of fear around this word, particularly perhaps because this was happening during the time when the Black Lives Matter movement was receiving a lot of publicity. The SPOC, from this place of fear, questioned whether what was happening in this area was actually 'racism' and wanted us to use a different term, like 'unconscious bias'.

This was a difficult situation. On one hand, we were sympathetic to the SPOC, who we had a very good relationship with. The researcher themself started to question whether it *was* racism. Did they have it wrong? On the other hand, we felt a commitment to tackling the structural and systemic harm that we had seen and documented through using the methods detailed in Part I. Drawing on our collective skills and experience (as described in Part II), we were able to address the situation. We – Rachael and Jenny – had a call with the researcher and went over the evidence. We talked through the researcher's own worries and what the SPOC might be concerned about. We created a plan for action. The researcher then spoke with the SPOC about what was worrying them and what would make them feel more comfortable. Ultimately, we were not prepared to remove the word 'racism', but we could help the SPOC understand why we thought this was the right thing to do. When the researcher spoke to the SPOC again, ahead of the review, she had in fact shifted her view and agreed that it should stay in – the preparation had helped her to reflect, and we were now aligned. The next week, the final system review was held, attended by professionals and senior directors. The research team went through the presentation and at two points the word 'racism' was used with direct quotes from what had been witnessed. Despite the SPOCs concerns and hesitations, nothing happened. No one baulked at the word; no one contested it. We'd love to say that this started a transformative conversation about racism and attitudes held in the area. But unfortunately, this book is about *real-life* system change. The reality is that it wasn't picked up or discussed by the site. In fact, it was ignored. And because the plans for action were shared between us and sites, we couldn't force them to prioritise the issue in their plan. We include this here as an example of system change work because, by using robust research methods alongside building strong relational trust, we provided an opportunity for this local authority to engage with structural racism. Even if they were not ready at this point to face these issues at a strategic level, the commitment of the SPOC and the team working in the school to addressing racism provided an incremental shift within the system that could be amplified and developed using the same methods, beyond our involvement.

Conclusion

When we started out on our road to system change, we didn't know what kinds of system changes the sites would end up with. We knew that we would be watched and assessed on our ability to improve the safety of young people in contexts beyond the home (as an aside, this is very hard to do and measure; Lloyd and Owens 2023). We knew it would be hard, that there would be considerable challenges and that it would be relationally and emotionally demanding. But we didn't know where the 'green shoots' would be, the 'aha' moments where we would get glimmers that our efforts were paying off. We also knew that we would be under pressure, as you probably are, to demonstrate the 'success' of our work even as we were still doing it; such is the nature of the context in which we work (Lefevre et al 2024). We have shared some examples of system change work in this chapter, but the reality is that most of the changes that happen, the outcomes that your work might lead to, are very likely to take place long after you have left. You may not get to see the changes you have inspired and the impact this has on those that are affected by the system – in our case, young people and families. So you need to find ways to sustain yourself in work that can feel, at times, hopeless. It is important to capture stories, big and small, on the difference your work has made. Noticing small shifts is important. Hearing about how your work has helped someone, even just one person, can make a big difference. We end by sharing some key pointers:

1. Create a way to record positive moments and impact you have. It might be a nice conversation you had with a professional. We stored these in our handover notes.
2. Trust your methods and relationships. If you're challenged on the grounds of saying something 'too sensitive', be patient and work with people so they understand your thinking, but ultimately you will likely need to find a way to be bold and say what needs to be said.
3. Remember that we're working in imperfect systems subject to many contextual challenges. The task is to keep this in mind while also holding a vision for what could be better. This requires a delicate balance of moving between dreaming and reality so that you can make some real-life changes.
4. If you are working in a place that seems to be culturally very different to your expectations and you're struggling to walk at the same pace, think about switching your approach. What works in one place might not work somewhere else. Above all, find ways to build relationships and tune in to what's going on and then work out your place from there.
5. Don't be shy about recognising the impact you're having, even if only among your team or with yourself. System change is partnership work, and of course the bulk of the groundwork of change in children's social care is done by those working day to day in systems, but the external researcher or systems change leader also has an important and unique role in activating change. It's important that you acknowledge this and notice when your work has an effect.

9

How theories can help us change systems

Introduction

In this book, we have referred to a few different theories and conceptual frameworks. In this chapter, we wanted to see if we could take things a little deeper and consider how these theoretical perspectives have shaped and informed the system change work we have done. Are there new models or ways of seeing problems that have emerged from this work? Are there new ways of integrating our existing ideas that could be helpful for us and others who go on to develop the approach? This chapter is an exploration of these questions. Not every one of our theoretical perspectives has been explicitly referenced in the book, but we want to show in this chapter how they have informed our thinking, ethics and feelings about the work we have done. In Chapter 1, we describe system change as a tree, with the trunk and branches being the methods and the roots, the relationships and cultures. Theories for us underpin this whole process; they are the soil in which the tree grows.

Many of the theories we used to do this work were ones we'd been steeped in for several years. We have been able to integrate them into our work and switch between them. They have served us well, particularly when it comes to grappling with ethical questions within our work and unpicking the trickier, more complex issues. There are the ideas that Contextual Safeguarding was founded on – these are the sociological ideas of Bourdieu

(1984) and the systems theorist Bronfenbrenner (1986). We've written about how these ideas helped us to approach not only extra-familial harm but also organisational contexts themselves as needing to be tackled contextually. In Chapter 7, we showed how these ideas helped us to contextualise problematic practice within organisations, helping us to not place blame on individual workers. Our system change is about trying to change professional conditions, just as we encourage practitioners to change social conditions for young people. Our thinking has also been influenced by the theoretical ideas of critical social work and social justice. For example, the work of writers such as Jan Fook (2014) has helped us when we talked about power and critiqued how individualistic ways of thinking tend to 'blame' those who are harmed rather than seeking to address the structural causes of harm, like poverty (Featherstone and Gupta 2018).

Alongside this, we have drawn on psychosocial ideas, particularly around the importance of paying attention to the emotional and relational aspects of organisational systems. We've been helped a great deal by the concept of system defences, which is the idea that anxiety gets played out within systems to create defensive practice in response to a set of untenable conditions related to the organisation's task (Menzies Lyth 1960). Another very helpful psychosocial idea is that of emotional containment, developed by the psychoanalyst, Bion (1962), and, for our purposes, its translation into organisational contexts (Ruch 2011). This is about how we all, but particularly those of us working in human services, experience individual and collective work-related anxieties which, if we are to function well, need to be held and 'metabolised' by the organisational systems that we work within. We saw an example of this right at the beginning of the book when, in Chapter 1, defending ourselves against the painful reality that a child had died and we hadn't been available for a professional, we questioned why they even wanted us to help. We've also explored how, as researchers, we might have a role in supporting emotional containment as well as encouraging it within the systems we're changing (Ruch et al 2016).

When it comes to research methodology, our work is based on a way of understanding knowledge production and meaning making as a pluralistic, shared, contingent and subjective endeavour. We talked about how we have been guided by the work of feminist researchers before us (for example, Oakley 2016) who recognised the need for researchers to be involved in the work they are doing, not standing aloof from it or treating research as a colonialist endeavour, extracting ideas from a superior position of expertise (Menzies 2004). We hope that in doing this, we have shown that theories are alive and doing important work within the system change approach we've developed.

Theories have helped us to make sense of things, explain things, understand what's going on, carry on and change things. Sometimes we have drawn on broad theoretical positions to help us in ways that may not have been so explicit in the writing. For instance, when we spoke in Chapter 8 about working from within systems, rather than seeking to abolish them we were drawing on critical realist ideas (Bhaskar 2013). This has helped us to adopt a position of pragmatic hopefulness that system change is possible. We continue to be interested in the idea of whether it's possible to work with the 'mechanisms' of a system in a meaningful way to uncover oppressive and empowering possibilities while also accepting that our understanding about these things will always be partial and contingent (Houston 2001). We could even say that the very idea that 'real life' 'exists', which is one of the basic working assumptions of this book, is supported by a critical real way of approaching 'reality', particularly within children's social care (Houston 2001). In this chapter, we focus specifically on how applying a psychosocial conceptualisation has helped us get at the 'real-life' aspects of system change. We end the chapter by presenting a multisystemic approach to embedded research.

Using psychosocial concepts for understanding systems

The main conceptual framework that we've drawn on in this book is a merging of sociological social constructionist ideas with psychoanalytic concepts in an integrated meta-theory called 'psychosocial'. Sociological, social constructionist ideas are critical of structural inequality, while psychoanalytic ideas are all about understanding human behaviour and development by looking at what's going on inside the human psyche. Social constructionist ideas support us to deconstruct how society is unequally structured, providing us with the means to think 'rationally' about what needs restructuring and to work towards a fairer distribution of resources; this aligns with social work's interest is 'power, difference and meaning' (McNamara 2009, p 162). Psychoanalytic theory provides a set of ideas for thinking deeply about the internal world of feelings, symbols and concepts. Where social construction is arguably in the realm of 'logic', psychoanalytic concepts are based on the idea of an unpredictable and dynamic unconscious (Woodward 2015) which contains 'raw' emotions, memories, 'thoughts' and feelings (Freud, cited in Preston-Shoot and Agass 1990). In many ways, these two theories seemingly oppose each other. Furthermore, several critiques have been levelled at psychoanalytic thinking and relationship-based practice by social constructionist, radical, critical and feminist theorists (for example, Brennan [1989]). Featherstone and Gupta (2018) suggest that relationship-based practice can create an individualistic and deterministic focus on the dynamic between a 'service user' and a practitioner that excludes context. Others have drawn attention to unethical practices such as the casual use of clinical material within psychoanalytic research (Archard and O'Reilly 2022), where the private lives of people in treatment are deconstructed for so called 'scholarly' purposes. We are alive to these critiques and have sought to keep them in mind, however, in using these theories, we draw on the many decades of work that has brought psychoanalytic and social constructionist ideas to bear on one another, and we believe that these can be usefully integrated into system change work.

We believe that to represent the complexity of real life, we need a complex set of theoretical ideas to hold us and help us make sense of the world. If we used only sociological, social constructionist ideas, we wouldn't have the tools we need to make sense of some of the 'beneath the surface' emotional experiences that exist within organisations, including our own research institution. But, on the other hand, if we used only psychoanalytic ideas, we could end up going down the route of implying that for young people and parents to be safe and have their needs met, all they need is a therapeutic relationship. We reject this idea (Cornell 2006), as we also reject the idea that safety can be created through 'fixing' young people's individual behaviour and 'choices' by changing their way of thinking (Owens and Lloyd 2023). The good news is that a psychosocial way of conceptualising the world allows us to weave together the 'internal' and 'external', the 'logical' and the 'irrational' in a way that doesn't set them up as binaries or opposites – we do not have to choose between the two (Clarke and Hoggett 2019).

Psychosocial thinking originated as a philosophical response to the horror and devastation caused by two world wars. Bringing together Marxist theory with psychoanalytic concepts offers a way of thinking that considers humans as both socially constructed within power structures and having internal emotional experiences (Frost 2019). Here the 'psycho' and the 'social' are ideologically (and linguistically) merged into a dynamic relationship with one another (Frosh 2003), offering a: '"rich" version of human experience in a constant and constituting relationship with their "environment" in the broadest sense, and as conflictual, bruised, affective, struggling, changing' (Frost 2019, p 2). A psychosocial conceptual framework therefore provides us with something that is close to 'real' in the sense that it seeks to take account of an experience of life as a constant, fluid and non-linear interaction between societal structures on the one hand and subjective experiences on the other (Redman 2016). This holding together of internal emotional experiences and external structured power networks was foundational for how we approached our work and wrote this book. We strongly believe that there is an 'out there' that needs reconstructing and an 'in here' that needs to be attended to, and that its vital to hold both in mind when doing embedded research for system change. In some ways, Part I attended more to the 'out there' of systems and Part II, the 'in here' of emotions. But, as we have been at pains to say, it is our belief that 'outer' and 'inner' is actually a false division: they should be integrated as much as possible if we want a rich and real-life way of thinking about and being in the world.

So how has this integration helped us understand and change systems? The specific concepts that have helped us most are those that have been used for thinking about groups and organisations rather than just individuals (Armstrong and Rustin 2015). One of these is 'object relations' theory (Klein 1952). Originally, this idea described the process of emotional and psychological development of a child, who, by receiving emotionally attuned love, care and attention from their primary carers, starts to 'take them in', psychically speaking. In object relations terms, a carer becomes a 'good internal object' (Ogden 1983) who can be drawn on throughout a person's life. This idea was then built on to think about how feelings and ideas transfer between people in ways that they are not always consciously aware of (Klein 1952).

Moving beyond individuals, the idea of 'group relations' takes these ideas and considers how the psychic interaction of people's unconscious processes impact how they behave in groups. Group relations, as a broad field of psychosocial study, has been particularly helpful in our work – for example, in supporting us to make sense of the experiences and behaviour of professionals working in organisations who might be facing pressure from both external neoliberal conditions and from the anxiety-provoking nature of safeguarding young people who are at extreme risk of death (Lefevre et al 2024). One of the ideas within group relations we draw on a lot is the idea of 'splitting' (Freud 1940) as applied to groups. When applied within organisational contexts, we can think about how when under pressure, teams can act defensively, creating a group identity around being the 'good team' – an identity which is dependent on seeing others as the 'bad team'. It is hard to imagine anyone who has ever worked in an organisation not immediately being able to recognise this phenomenon. Splitting can be used to understand why there is so much siloed working and hard boundaries around service areas, despite decades of serious case reviews that say that teams and agencies need to be better at working *together*. An example of this that comes up time and time again in our work is the division between statutory social care services and voluntary and community sector organisations. For those not working in this area, an unnuanced summary might be: youth work can see statutory services as 'detached' from the realities of young people's lives, and social workers might prioritise 'statutory' agencies and not value the contributions of youth work, maybe considering them to be 'unboundaried' or less professional in their approach when in fact both voluntary and statutory agencies have important and complementary roles to play. In our work to change the way that systems respond to extra-familial harm, we used the idea of splitting to help us understand the 'blockages' in systems and also to think about how parents can become the focus of blame, setting up a 'good system'/'bad parent' dynamic. For example, in one site, the narrative of the 'bad' parent had become so embedded in the history and culture of how social work engaged with parents that even when children were exploited in situations that had nothing to do with their families, social workers continued to find ways to discuss how parents were complicit and involved.

The good thing about doing embedded research is that you should have time built in to take a step back, get some perspective and think about what might be going on. Taking time for analysis can provide a way to understand, and hopefully reduce, the splitting that might be going on by allowing time to think about where it might be coming from. We need to look carefully at the intolerable situations and feelings that organisations and teams are facing (like not knowing how to help young people facing extreme suffering). Doing this can help us to understand what function it serves teams to disavow their own difficult feelings and instead attribute them to others (this is known as 'projection'; Knight 1940). We need to be curious about the conditions that have led to the fantasy creation of the 'bad' other and the needs being met in the creation of the 'good' self. As researchers, it is also very important that we try to avoid getting caught up in splitting ourselves. This can happen when we create the idea that one part of the system or person is just 'bad' and we, in opposition, are just 'good' researchers.

Another theory that we have drawn on within the field of group relations that links to 'splitting' is the idea of emotional containment within systems (Bion 1962). In Chapter 5, we outline how containment is something that can also take place between a researcher and research participants (Menzies Lyth 1960) and discuss the role of reflection and reflexive discussion within our team to support us to be able to offer containment. Building in ways to process and hold anxiety for others and within our team has helped us avoid splitting and defensive practice by allowing us to notice when feelings might be being 'transferred' from our sites of study and learn from this. Importantly, though, a supportive researcher can never ameliorate the sorts of pressures faced by people working in children's social care, and nor are they expected to. This is where we must ensure that the 'social' in psychosocial has its place. This could include reflecting back to practitioners and managers your observations about the way the system is currently operating and your understanding of why this is. You might recommend that service leaders invest in safe, emotionally containing reflective spaces. Alongside this, you might engage in activism and advocacy at a national policy level to seek to alter the structural conditions that create intolerable pressures within the system.

Returning to the example of practice that blames 'bad' parents, part of your response to this splitting might be to develop tools for practitioners that help them identify the contextual nature of harm (such as poverty) – for example, rather than seeing parents as complicit in harm, understanding the conditions that might make it hard for parents to control the circumstances beyond their front doors. Then, even if workers have no input into housing or finances, their parenting assessments would be able to correctly name the source of stress within families rather than resorting to an idea of 'neglectful parents'; this could potentially bring about relationships between practitioners and families characterised by solidarity rather than blame (Reynolds 2011) and enable them to focus their efforts on advocating for better housing and finacial support. As Frost (2019, p 3) writes:

> Poverty, and the callous contemporary benefits systems which instigates and reinforces this, certainly limits opportunities, guarantees substandard living, and endless hardship. However, it also engenders shame, anxiety, and a sense of worthlessness. No one should have to feel shamed for what is outside their control, but research and practice understands that people do.

We think it is unfair that people enter a profession like social work expecting to empower and help people only to find that they are agents of a punitive state and conditioned into enacting these limiting, shaming processes. It is the collective work of families, practitioners and researchers to change these systems locally and nationally, but the starting point is seeing this for what it is, and much of our system change work has simply been about this – seeing things for what they are. Finding a more 'real-life' and honest way of looking at things that is better for those who deliver and those who 'receive' services. For us, the value of a psychosocial approach is that there is room to understand and change systems in a way that honours the interchangeable nature of emotional and structural needs.

Many therapeutic modalities are based on the idea that rather than being subject to our feelings and reactions to life's difficulties, we can become aware of them through reflective discussion within a safe and supportive relationship and, in so doing, arrive at a better understanding of ourselves and how we relate to others. Alongside this, sociological approaches engage us in a process of 'conscientisation' (Freire 1970) to become more aware of how society is unfairly structured according to power and privilege. We hold both these ideas together, believing that it is important to reflect on one's emotional experiences and how these might be played out in groups and organisations and also, importantly, be aware of the broader structures and systems in which these emotions and experiences are formed. Being able to take a wider view of the system, to understand it from many directions and to explain this to those who are involved day to day can be very powerful. We saw examples of this in our work – like in Chapter 7 when Jenny plucked up the courage to share the findings of her case file review and, though it was hard to hear, the people working in that system were glad to know. As system change researchers, we have the opportunity to help people see their systems differently and make sense of their experiences within them. To do this, we need a broad theoretical lens that can take in the complex, multifaced world of children's social care and human systems. Having a way to understand and see what's going on is the first stage of being able to make changes.

Multisystemic thinking

One of the underpinning ideas behind psychosocial concepts is the idea that all of life – be it individually and in groups, internally and externally, psychically and socially – is interconnected within a dynamic system. In this book, we use the word 'system' a lot. We talk about 'the social care system' and 'system change'. When we use a broad psychosocial conceptualisation of life, what does that do for the idea of 'system'? How can we apply these theories to the notion of embedded research? The field of psychosocial studies is relatively new and there is more to be explored, beyond the idea of intra-personal processes being applied to groups (Redman 2016). In this part of the chapter, we look at how our system change work could contribute to a transdisciplinary theoretical view of human systems and system change through the integration of our experiences of doing system change work as embedded researchers.

Often in system change theory, we hear about the idea of a 'theory of change' (Weiss 1995). Sometimes, this can be treated like a linear formula – if we do x then y will (hopefully) happen. The idea of change is particularly relevant for social work, where the question of how people change is central to the work: 'Why don't (some) people change, when it seems to be in their best interests' is perhaps a classic response of the first placement social work student, grounded either in positivist psychology, or indeed postmodern inflected sociology which ascribes a great deal of agency to individuals' (Ferguson, cited in Frost 2019). Our work in Contextual Safeguarding involved turning on its head the question of how people in organisations change and helping people to understand that individual 'agency' is contingent on context rather than being a 'rational tool for personal change or action at will ... [and] similarly [it is not] (wilfully) switched off' (Frost 2019, p 120). Bringing this broader understanding of how a person acts in relation to their environment together with a psychosocial formulation of inner emotional worlds brings us to a different way of approaching change. Rather than thinking about whether it is structure *or* agency that enables change, a psychosocial framework allows us to see these things as interdependent. It allows us to approach the idea of change through a multi-dimensional lens. What we mean by this is that the only way to bring about change is with an awareness of life as a complex, interactive and multi-dimensional system.

When she was developing Contextual Safeguarding, Carlene Firmin expanded the ecological model of Bronfenbrenner (1986) to include extra-familial contexts. Bronfenbrenner's model has been drawn upon many times. Wilson (2008), for example, conceptualises the relationship between a social worker and a service user to show how two different organisational and personal systems are nested within a wider social-cultural environment.

Figure 9.1: Multisystems in embedded research

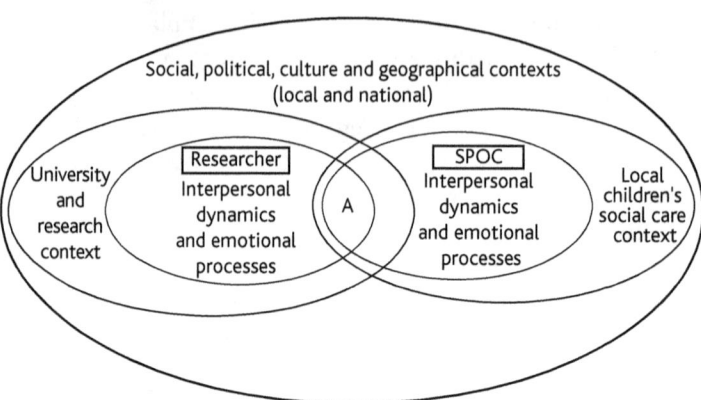

More recently, work in the field of multisystemic resilience has used the ecological model to conceptulise how geo-socio-eco-psycho systems interrelate and are nested within one another, opening up much-needed space for 'diverse sources of knowledge and world views […] including those that indigenize and decolonize knowledge as well as those that challenge discourses that privilege certain genders, abilities and racial biases' (Ungar 2021, p 4).

Building on all of these, we have also adapted the ecological model to conceptualise the approach described in this book and homed in on in this chapter. In Figure 9.1, we represent our understanding of multisystemic processes for embedded research that brings together ecological approaches to systems with a psychosocial lens to emotions and relationships. Our theory of change is grounded in the idea that the systems contained within this model are not discreet or separate but are in constant flux and flow between one another. Figure 9.1 includes three spheres. The outermost sphere includes the social, political, cultural and geographical contexts, which are, of course, extremely complex and multifaceted. However, we have simplified them here to broadly encapsulate the larger structures that researchers and professionals exist within. In the next sphere, we have used the examples of a researcher and SPOC for ease, but this could be people with different roles within embedded research. Within this sphere is the university research context where if you are an embedded researcher from an academic institution, you will be situated. If you are perhaps from a think tank or charity instead, this would be the institutional context you are situated in. Also within this sphere is the local children's social care context. This is the organisation you are trying to change. These two organisational spaces intercept. You – the embedded researcher – will of course be situated within the local organisational context, but the organisation will also be drawn into your institution's sphere through research, working culture, publishing and learning. In the central sphere is the interpersonal, emotional system. We have added this sphere to the more traditional ecological models to represent the significance of the 'inner world' impacts of being emotional and psychological beings. If there is anything we have been trying to show throughout this book, it is that researchers and SPOCs, as humans in real life, are subject to feelings and relationships that are in dynamic interaction, and what happens between them can ripple out and inform what takes place in other spheres within the multi-dimensional system that they sit within.

This may sound rather grand, but the place where all spheres converge is point A. This is where the embedded researcher encounters the SPOC, and through their dynamic reflective relationship, they have access to the multiple perspectives that their systems provide. Point A is a portal through which we can draw on many converging ways of understanding what is 'going on' in a system and how to change it. Obviously, like any model, this one has its limits. There are multiple systems collapsed into the outside sphere, including the experiences of young people and families in terms of how they interact with services and their lives beyond this. However, we offer this model as a 'good enough' reflection of how change within children's social care involves a fluid engagement with interactive multi-dimensional systems.

It is not simply that we are *aware* of the many system levels. This book has been about how we can *tune into* the specific nature of the elements of the system you are working within. We learn about them through forming relationships. But it is not only awareness that is important; through embedded research, we enter into a dynamic relationship with the people in our sites; our interpersonal emotional systems interact, and it is through this that we can make change happen. When we trained 'champions' in

Contextual Safeguarding right at the start of the project, we didn't just want them to learn about the system and concept – we wanted them to like us. We made jokes, we engaged in playful exchanges and got to know people, because we knew on some level that this is how you make change happen. If we can be excused the rather grand claim, it is through this that we have made change at a social and political scale. At the time of writing, the Department for Education are funding a trial of the Risk Outside the Home pathway (Firmin 2024) that was piloted in one site. It is likely that a version of this will enter statutory English policy. This didn't come from nowhere. It was formed in the seeds that were sown when we clambered into the back of one practitioner's car as she made excuses about the mess. It was grown in the meetings where we shared cupcakes baked by another. It was tendered to, carefully, over multiple meetings to reassure and support. This is where system change happens.

Conclusion

Using embedded research to change systems can feel like many things. Occasionally, it can be rewarding, as we explored in Chapter 8. Other times, it can be very confronting and take us out of our comfort zones. But most of the time, building and growing relationships with individuals within complex systems is intense – sometimes enjoyably so, sometimes overwhelmingly so. Even when we are sitting in an office with nothing to do, while we might feel a bit lost or bored at one level, on another level we have millions of questions going round our heads about the people around us, how we feel about being involved in research, how they feel about us, what dictates the decisions they are making and the way they are acting. This is where the ideas in this chapter can come in. There is probably no way to get around the intensity of embedded research. We have been enormously helped however, by having access to a multiperspectival lens, where we have been able to hold in mind, and then work with, unconscious emotional processes alongside sociological and structural theories. Working in this way has helped us to take a step back, and just as we might deliver a review to people in sites about what is going on, we can do this for ourselves. When we look at Figure 9.1, we can see that what we are trying to do is quite a lot. It is ambitious and complex (and the figure actually simplifies a great deal). So we end once again with some key pointers to help you keep going:

1. If you feel emotional and overwhelmed, remember that you are engaged in a complex psychosocial task.
2. We've said it before, but it can't be said enough – you need reflective support with colleagues that can help you share your feelings but also help you use theories to understand what is 'going on'.
3. Understanding what is going on is the first step to change, and what is going on won't be straightforward or simple, but very complex.
4. Use the multisystemic psychosocial ideas to 'zoom in' or 'zoom out' during reflections to help you consider things from different perspectives.
5. Remember that splitting, defences and other processes like this are not 'bad' – they are things that we do to cope. So if you spot them, work gently towards reducing the need for them in your system.

10

Conclusion

Introduction

We begin this chapter with two poems. The first, 'The ending', is about our experiences of running our final project event. During the event, as the poem describes, we asked people to make creative work as part of a reflective activity about the four-year project. The second poem, 'It's been bloody hard work but …', is an example of something that was written and read out by one of the groups at the event.

The ending

That morning started nervous   slow
In this grand gilded hotel ballroom
                    Strange and vast
So different from the unlit municipal offices and back rooms
The Teams calls   and then the bedrooms
Where we met each other   these three years
Week in   week out
        Thinking   talking   imagining   together

With Covid still in the air   they came   in twos and threes
Bringing out their phones to show that they were safe
We greeted with warm hellos but
They huddled
              around their tables

Conclusion

                    unsure what it was we'd invited them to
Not wanting to feel exposed
Seeming shy

It was a beautiful unfolding
                a gradual thawing
To start, a gentle invitation to reflect
                      use these 'Post-it notes' –
                      remember them?
Tell us about the good things the hard things the messy things

Then   with a giddy giggle   people mixed up
                   started
talking   sharing
We said make something   a poem   a song   a little drama (wondering will it work?)
Tell us what it's been like
We want to know

And they exploded in
idiosyncratic   radiant colour
Four groups   four extraordinary creative offerings that
                  made us laugh
                  made us weep
Yes, they said, we'll tell you
It's been amazing and hard and brilliant
and yes, hard

Yes   and now its ending
Yes   we said
And because we like to laugh   w e   g a v e
                                    them awards
Silly but serious
Made-up awards that show that we noticed them
We noticed   and care

It's been bloody hard work but ...

So many pressures, so little time
Trying to make sure young people are fine
COVID, re-organisations, and changes galore
But one thing's for sure – we've got to do more!

Partnership buy-in is a definite must
Some of us are struggling to build up that trust
A cultural shift its small steps we take
But when we get it right – what a difference we make

Contextual conferencing and business surveys
How to get partners to change their ways
Youth workers out and communities in
So many PowerPoints   we almost gave in

Some glimmers and differences in our approach
For all of us – the role of social work, we've had to broach
We're still on a journey, we're still travelling
But at the end of the day, its
CONTEXTUAL SAFEGUARDING

Introduction

We wrote this book to explore and share the possibilities that are open to us when we ditch idealistic notions of perfect processes in system change. Instead, we embrace system change as a complex, messy, multilayered, energetic activity – in other words, something that is much closer to 'real life'. In practical terms, for us, this has meant using systematic data collection methods alongside getting stuck in with people in systems – building relationships with them and alongside this using psychosocial ideas to reflect on the richness of what is 'going on'. We hope you have found this book both inspiring and accessible with practical tools and clear guidelines for methods you can pick up and adapt for your own work. We also hope you feel clear about how these methods need to be set within the real-life context where you are working.

An important element of navigating and honouring this is to develop respectful relationships with those working in the system, especially with the person leading the work, who we have called the SPOC. We hope you feel ready to centre these relationships in your work and understand them as the life force of change.

Our approach is a hybrid method to systems change, drawing on embedded research methods as an emerging social science concept and practice (McGinity and Salokangas 2014) along with psychosocial contributions to organisational research (Cooper 2009). We don't offer a step-by-step formula to achieve change, but neither is our approach the same as that of the organisational consultant within the psychoanalytic tradition (Long 2001). As we explore at the end of this chapter, the beauty of the real-life approach that we have set out is that it integrates methods for 'doing', methods for 'feeling' and methods for 'thinking', giving each value and importance within system change work. We believe that this reflects how life is lived and experienced – that is, as a set of intersubjective relationships that are situated within highly structured social and political systems and which are subject to cultural forces and unconscious feelings, many of which are completely out of our immediate awareness. However, we believe that by taking in this 'as full as possible' version of organisational life in all its complexity and accepting that our ability to make changes within this context will always be conditional and partial, we can enter system change work, get stuck in and do great things.

Context is everything, and so in this concluding chapter, we contextualise our method further by sharing what we learnt about doing system change in different places and the way that local differences can shape what happens. We explore what it means to end a system change project and what happens next, looking at how our learning through the Scale-Up project influenced later work. We end the chapter by stepping back and looking at the core elements of the real-life approach, providing a broad model for you to take with you and anchor you in your own work.

The impact of regional differences on system change

The five UK and four subsequent London sites in the Scale-Up project were, as we explained in Chapter 1, recruited through an application process. Carlene Firmin, who led the project (as the principal investigator), visited the shortlisted places. Foremost in her mind was the local commitment in each area to mobilise system change, and each of the sites chosen demonstrated their potential for this. As the initial Contextual Safeguarding implementation was in the London Borough of Hackney, the Scale-Up project was interested in the effects of developing equivalent systems in places with different demographics to Hackney, which is an inner city, ethnically diverse borough with a particular relationship to social work innovation (Goodman et al 2011). With this in mind, the sites were chosen to provide social, cultural, political and geographical contrast, representing areas across southern and northern England and Wales, urban and coastal cities, large rural counties and industrial suburban areas. Right from the start, the differences between the sites were very clear. Here is vignette of a memory which marks this out for Rachael:

RESEARCHER REFLECTION

During the set-up of the project we travelled on consecutive days to two sites for the initial setting-up meetings. The meeting in the first site was held in an affluent market town (there was a Pret A Manger nearby!). The meeting itself was in a wooden-panelled council building with pictures on the walls of grand-looking people. A select group of senior people had been invited. I remember thinking that I was glad that I had a dress on because I fitted in. The next day we travelled a long way to the other site to do the same thing. When we arrived at the rural seaside city, our taxi took us a long way from the centre to a well-loved youth centre set in an estate. Suddenly I felt self-conscious of my dress and I began to realise that my decision to pack light had been a mistake. I felt very out of place in the youth centre with everyone else in casual clothes. I kept thinking, 'I wonder what they think of me', the university researcher, looking so smart and out of touch.

Although on this occasion Rachael might have felt a bit out of place in a dress, the feelings she had about the different cultures of these two places show that we had chosen well in terms of contrasting contexts. Over time, as the project developed, we learnt to tune in and adapt our way of working in the different places. This went far beyond just wearing the right things so as not to stand out; it involved us adapting our research methods and tools, often in situ (Schön 2017). A reflection of our need to adapt to the culture of sites can be seen in the different approaches we took to planning our data collection visits. While one site would send a packed schedule of meetings and line us up with a long list of people to act as host, others would seem to have forgotten we were coming but when we reminded them, would be able to send someone quite senior to meet us, who would then spend the rest of the day with us, explaining how things worked there and the history and culture. So we worked out quite quickly we could learn about the sites through these adaptations. Sometimes, it meant we were just sitting in an office and seeing what was going on. While this might not have been part of our plan for the day, we often learnt a great deal and generated very valuable 'data' by observing how people interacted in an office and through impromptu invites to meetings from people seeing us sitting there and looking a little lost! So having a flexible approach to your data collection plan can lead to some really valuable learning.

During the project, we also learnt about the impact of changing systems in areas where there have been many years of intergenerational poverty. We have worked in many places where the context of neoliberal policies has individualised the idea of 'change', so that it is treated as something that is the responsibility held by people who experience hardship, rather than systems (Strier and Binyamin 2010). This was particularly prevalent in one of the sites we worked with, and we saw how this had led to a culture of compartmentalising young people and parents as 'good' or 'bad' as a way to manage this. In a context like this, we saw how it could be easy to drive through change at one level, but miss the need to go deeper and support the system to reconnect to the values and legislative frameworks that underpin children's social care – that is, working collaboratively with parents and promoting children's rights.

Finally, one of the most significant things we learnt about local context and system change relates to the stability of the workforce. A group of people who have stayed around in a place, especially a small place, tend to form good relationships, tend to be invested in each other. We found that some of the most successful long-term changes were possible in those contexts. This isn't to say that it's not possible to make changes elsewhere – of course it is – but because the energy that is needed to get system change going often revolves around a single person, the SPOC; when the SPOC leaves their post, this can have a destabilising effect on the change process. Long term success relies to a large extent, on how much it's been possible to share responsibility for the change beyond the SPOC. This has important implications for how we end a system change project, as we explore next.

Endings

As a society, and in organisational system change, we tend to neglect thinking about endings (Gilmore 2000). They can be awkward and painful, but over time we have learnt how important they are, especially with a methodology like ours, which is so reliant on relationships. But what is a good way to end embedded research projects, and how do we negotiate the process of embedding, ensuring ongoing fidelity alongside moving on and letting go?

How do you let go?

Our first experiences of ending embedded research projects were mixed. Rachael remembers feelings of guilt around ending her first embedded project. She had the feeling that she was somehow abandoning the practitioners to their very complex work, no longer being available to be that listening ear and (hopefully) supportive presence. Not long after she left, the project folded unexpectedly, and she had an even stronger sense of concern. She also struggled to know how far she should keep in touch, plagued by ideas about boundaries and fairness. Endings are complicated, and although we shouldn't assume that we are integral to the running of the teams we've been part of, neither should we deny the role we've had. If we think back to Figure 9.1, we have, to a large extent, inserted ourselves *into* a system and become part of

Conclusion

it, so removing ourselves will cause some readjustments on either side, and sometimes this can feel quite painful.

Our endings in the Scale-Up project were not perfect, but there is no such thing. There was considerable turbulence created by the ongoing impact of COVID-19, a shift within our research team's own institutional context and the inevitable staff changes that occur as projects come towards the end of their term. But in the midst of this, we did think carefully about marking the ending. Our endings were staged: in each site, there was a final system review, where we summed up the changes that were made against the individual site plans. We left each site with some final reflections on embedding and explained that our work would now shift away from regular contact to developing resources for dissemination. We also invited everyone who had been involved in the project to attend an event where we employed external facilitators to run a reflective workshop (as described in the poems at the start of this chapter). We were led in creative activities, where people explored questions about what we had learnt, what went well, what we were most proud of and what the challenges were. Although at the start of the day, there was an air of nervousness (heightened by the recent lockdown), by the end of the morning session, small groups had shared mini-dramas, poems and told stories about their experiences. We ended the morning with an 'awards ceremony'. The sharing sessions had been heartfelt, fun but also serious, and we wanted to take a similar tone with our final collective conversation. We wanted to thank people but in a way that was meaningful and showed that we noticed their differences and the ways they'd not only contributed to the overall project but also made our lives richer. The awards ranged from silly things like 'the person most likely to be on four different online calls at the same time while also being on a call with us' to more serious things like 'biggest champion of Contextual Safeguarding'. We tried to give it a bit of glamour by using gold envelopes and inviting people up to receive their awards.

After the event, we also held more intimate goodbye meetings where research leads met with SPOCs. By the time the Scale-Up project ended, our meetings with SPOCs looked quite different in each of the sites. For example, in one site, the last meeting involved a methodical retrospective of the project, looking in detail at the plan and celebrating the wins, while in another site, the last meeting involved sharing stories about the momentum that was building and changes that were being made. Inevitably, some endings were fractured and less smooth; we found it hard to let go and were unsure how to. In one final meeting, a SPOC told the lead researcher that she was changing her role, leaving the researcher wondering if all their hard work would quickly unravel. Letting go can be hard when we are invested in the outcome and feel that if we could just get to a certain point, which is tantalisingly close, then things would be much more stable. To manage these feelings, we came back to the real-life mantra of accepting that there is no perfect time to end. This doesn't mean we would just stop and run off, but neither should we hold a project open indefinitely. We have learnt that keeping to a flexible but firm ending is helpful. Alongside this, we recommend talking about what the ending means rather than avoiding it. Invent some 'rituals' (like the awards ceremony). Certainly, for us, these things helped us to manage the difficult feelings and support everyone, including ourselves, through the process.

Fidelity and what happens next

System change never really ends: systems are always evolving, always shifting and changing. But, in reality, researchers or project leaders have a finite amount of time in which to bring about change within a particular system. For us, the initial project took place over four years, which is a relatively long amount of time to have dedicated to working on changing a system. You might have quite a bit less. So how do we plan for and take into account the inevitable sense that our work is not really complete, that there is always more to do? When we started out on our work, we had a neat four-year plan – setting up the project in the first year, then spending the second year scoping and planning, the third year testing and the final year embedding. In each of the sites we worked with (four in London and five in the rest of the UK), we hoped that when we ended there would be something that would resemble a Contextual Safeguarding system in each place. Of course, we hadn't reckoned on a global pandemic; nevertheless, in reality, the extent of the shift varied a great deal: in some places,

Conclusion

there were completely new Contextual Safeguarding teams in place and new partnerships established, but at the other end of the scale, there were those sites who had tried a few new things, like a single context assessment, but who had hit some brick walls and were left with more questions than answers. Most sites were somewhere in between, with many new positive 'green shoots' around shifts in structures and cultures that were beginning to take hold, which left us feeling optimistic but also worried about what would happen next.

One of the hardest parts of bringing in a new system is the question of 'fidelity', which is the extent to which an approach is being implemented as it was intended (Hall et al 2024). Contextual Safeguarding is not a model; there are not strict rules around how it should be 'delivered' (Firmin 2020). Rather, it has been developed in partnership with practitioners in sites who have tested its implementation as part of an iterative process. Having said this, there are some aspects of the approach that must be incorporated – those things that make it uniquely Contextual Safeguarding – so there *are* boundaries around what it is and what it is not. During the project, we had opportunity to influence, reflect on and give feedback on the extent to which the changes that sites made were aligned with the domains and values of Contextual Safeguarding. Of course, our influence was mitigated by many things, but it was still a live process of working out together. One of the most confronting aspects of ending the Scale-Up project was letting go of that influence and the reflective space that could help ensure that the systems we had set on track would continue to grow in a way that was faithful to their original design. Another worry was that the initial work would just fizzle away, that the little green shoots would not amount to anything – they would be eaten up by the 'slugs' of many other demands and the return of the dominant cultures and structures we'd been working so hard to shift. This was a worry we know was shared by some SPOCs and other key people in the sites who were part of the Scale-Up project – that once the energy and momentum created by having an external research team had gone, people would move on, taking the knowledge, experience and influence with them.

We don't have any magical solutions to these things. Alongside learning about and embedding system change, we learnt a great deal during Scale-Up about the challenges of changing systems. We gained a deeper understanding, for example, of the cultural issues that underlie a blaming approach to parents and young people (Thornhill 2023). We saw how the uncertain policy and practice climate around extra-familial harm could lead to new forms of surveillance over young people and new forms of data sharing that had little to do with relationships of trust and the aims of Contextual Safeguarding (Wroe and Manister 2024). When we finished the Scale-Up project, we were left with a strong sense of responsibility, not just to maintain relationships with the sites we'd spent such a lot of time developing systems with, but also to the wider sector, where there is increasing interest in the Contextual Safeguarding approach. We understand that our situation is perhaps different from yours, but you may also find yourself left with some big questions which circle around opportunities and challenges once your project is over. For us, it was important that we used these questions to shape what we did next. We put our efforts into preparing a toolkit to support others seeking to follow the process that we took during the Scale-Up project. This was a complete 'how to' guide to creating Contextual Safeguarding systems (Contextual Safeguarding 2022b). Through this toolkit, we have tried to address the challenges of system change, ethics and fidelity we were confronted with when analysing our data.

Following from this, we also developed new focused research projects looking at some of the specific challenges that came up, including projects on: the sustainability of the social work role when doing Contextual Safeguarding (Owens 2024); the question of school exclusions and extra-familial harm (Lloyd 2024); the advancement of a specific child protection pathway for extra-familial harm (Firmin 2024); and inequalities within systems designed to respond to young people's experiences of extra-familial harm (Wroe 2024). We share these things in the hope that you will be inspired to think about how you can weave the threads from your system change work into what happens next. This is less about ensuring fidelity and more about honouring the process you started, taking time to pay attention to what you have learnt and what you need to integrate into the next work you do, in a way that keeps you connected but also allows you to let go.

Conclusion

When we first started thinking about writing this book and working out what we wanted to say, we thought about what we'd done in terms of 'feeling', 'thinking' and 'doing'. These three words seemed to sum up for us the processes that had characterised our work, processes that were very intertwined, so much so that it would be more accurate to say feelingthinkingdoing. This echoes the writer Liz Berry's (2018) use of squashed words in her poem 'The republic of motherhood', where she describes the mother's task as 'Feedingcleaninglovingfeeding' to denote the intensity and permeable nature of these tasks. However, whilst on a day to day basis 'feeling', 'thinking' and 'doing' were all squashed together, for the purposes of writing this book we have broadly mapped them out in this way: in Part I, we mostly concentrate on the 'doing' of system change; in Part II, we turn to 'feeling'; and then, in Part III, we do some 'thinking'. But, of course, there is 'doing' in the 'feeling', 'feeling' in the 'doing', and 'thinking' in all parts. So these three things together can form a kind of virtuous triangle — a flow of processes that inform, spark and deepen the learning that's going on.

One of the most important messages that we would like to underline as we conclude this book is that system change is a multifaceted, complex process, involving human emotion, relationships and cultures, set within structures and systems in a constant state of social and political flux. Basically, if your system change work feels like you are in a whirlwind at times, then you are very likely getting at the heart of this complexity and doing a good job. If you find system change straightforward, if you have no challenges, if people do what you suggest and there is nothing that you don't understand, then you're probably missing something really important or, rather, missing a way of engaging your system that is crucial to its future development. Furthermore, if you find yourself getting consumed with singling out 'bad practice' and frustrated at individuals, you are losing sight of the structural nature of systems and the way that strong feelings, especially anxiety, plays out in organisational processes. It's important to take a step back and ask yourself: what power, structures, systems, relationships, emotions and cultures contribute to what is happening here? It is through these questions that we can start to get closer to what is 'really' going on within the systems we are working with.

Whirlwinds are exhilarating and exciting, but the reason why we describe the methods in Part I is that you also need some grounding, something to *do* that isn't just hanging around an office trying not to be weird! Our experience of following this 'feelingthinkingdoing' approach – combining practical tools with relational and emotional engagement and regularly holding reflective discussions and writing – is very rewarding and can lead to many unexpected outcomes. There is a kind of everyday magic that can happen when you combine these things, when you tolerate the unpredictability and mess and let yourself be contained by the process, trusting that it will lead to system change even if you don't yet know exactly what that will be. Human systems are so dynamic, children's social care especially so, due to the high levels of human suffering, government scrutiny and public ambivalence about its task. Making changes will never be straightforward, but we firmly believe that if you take a real-life attitude, it can be done.

References

Ahmed, S. (2000). 'Whose counting?' *Feminist Theory* **1**(1): 97–103.
Ahmed, S. (2013). *The Cultural Politics of Emotion*, New York: Routledge.
Archard, P.J. and M. O'Reilly (2022). 'Psychoanalytic therapy and narrative research interviewing: some reflections', *Nurse Researcher* 30.
Armstrong, D. and M. Rustin (2015). 'Introduction: Revisiting the paradigm', in D. Armstrong and M. Rustin (eds) *Social Defences against Anxiety*, London: Routledge: 1–23.
Atkinson, P.E. (1990). *Creating Culture Change*, Bedford: IFS.
Auden, W.H. (1938). 'Musée des Beaux Arts'. Retrieved 1 February 2024, from https://english.emory.edu/classes/paintings&poems/auden.html
Baars, S. (2014). 'The retreat of the state and the future of social science', *Management in Education* **28**(1): 6–11.
BBC (2024). 'Bereaved families call for change in anonymity law'. Retrieved 5 March 2024, from www.bbc.co.uk/news/articles/cd1dx9p41lwo
Beckett, H., I. Brodie, F. Factor, M. Melrose, J. Pearce, J. Pitts, L. et al (2013). *'It's Wrong-but You Get Used to It': A Qualitative Study of Gang-Associated Sexual Violence Towards, and Exploitation of, Young People in England*, Luton: University of Bedfordshire.
Bernard, C. and P. Harris (2016). *Safeguarding Black Children: Good Practice in Child Protection*, London: Jessica Kingsley Publishers.
Berry, L. (2018). *The Republic of Motherhood*, London: Random House.
Bhaskar, R. (2013). *A Realist Theory of Science*, London: Routledge.
Bigby, C., M. Knox, J. Beadle-Brown and T. Clement (2015). '"We just call them people": positive regard as a dimension of culture in group homes for people with severe intellectual disability', *Journal of Applied Research in Intellectual Disabilities* **28**(4): 283–295.

Bion, W.R. (1962). *Learning from Experience*, London: Heinemann.

Bondi, L. (2003). 'Empathy and identification: conceptual resources for feminist fieldwork', *ACME: An International Journal for Critical Geographies* **2**(1): 64–76.

Bourdieu, P. (1984). *Distinction: A Social Critique of the Judgement of Taste*, Cambridge, MA: Harvard University Press.

Bradbury, H. and B.M.B. Lichtenstein (2000). 'Relationality in organizational research: exploring the space between', *Organization Science* **11**(5): 551–564.

Braithwaite, J. (1989). *Crime, Shame and Reintegration*, Cambridge: Cambridge University Press.

Brennan, T. (1989). *Between Feminism and Psychoanalysis*, London: Routledge.

Bronfenbrenner, U. (1979). *The Ecology of Human Development: Experiments by Design and Nature*, Cambridge, MA: Harvard University Press.

Bronfenbrenner, U. (1986). 'Ecology of the family as a context for human development: research perspectives', *Developmental Psychology* **22**(6): 723–742.

Case, S. and T. Bateman (2020). 'The punitive transition in youth justice: reconstructing the child as offender', *Children & Society* **34**(6): 475–491.

Cheetham, M., A. Wiseman, B. Khazaeli, E. Gibson, P. Gray, P. Van der Graaf et al (2018). 'Embedded research: a promising way to create evidence-informed impact in public health?', *Journal of Public Health* **40**(suppl 1): i64–i70.

Clarke, S. and P. Hoggett (2019). 'Researching beneath the surface: a psycho-social approach to research practice and method', in S. Clarke and P. Hoggett (eds) *Researching Beneath the Surface*, Abingdon: Routledge: 1–26.

Cockbain, E. and K. Olver (2019). 'Child trafficking: characteristics, complexities, and challenges', in I. Bryce, Y. Robinson and W. Petherick (eds) *Child Abuse and Neglect*, London: Academic Press: 95–116.

Contextual Safeguarding (2022a). 'System review tools'. Retrieved 7 February 2024, from www.contextualsafeguarding.org.uk/resources/toolkit-overview/system-review/

References

Contextual Safeguarding (2022b). 'The Scale-Up toolkit'. Retrieved 1 February 2024, from www.contextualsafeguarding.org.uk/toolkits/scale-up-toolkit/

Contextual Safeguarding Network (2021). 'Beyond referrals – schools'. Retrieved 29 June 2021, from www.csnetwork.org.uk/en/beyond-referrals-levers-for-addressing-harmful-sexual-behaviour-in-schools

Cooper, A. (2009). 'Hearing the grass grow: emotional and epistemological challenges of practice-near research', *Journal of Social Work Practice* **23**(4): 429–442.

Cooper, A. (2018). *Conjunctions: Social Work, Psychoanalysis and Society*, Abingdon: Routledge.

Cornell, K.L. (2006). 'Person-in-situation: history, theory, and new directions for social work practice', *Praxis* 6(4): 50–57.

Cyr, J. (2016). 'The pitfalls and promise of focus groups as a data collection method', *Sociological Methods & Research* **45**(2): 231–259.

Davis, J. and N. Marsh (2022). 'The myth of the universal child', in D. Holmes (ed) *Safeguarding Young People: Risk, Rights, Resilience and Relationships*, London: Jessica Kingsley Publishers: 111–128.

Department for Education (2023). *Children's Social Care: Stable Homes, Built on Love*, London: Secretary of State for Education.

Dowling, R. (2005). 'Power, subjectivity and ethics in qualitative research', in I. Hay (ed) *Qualitative Research Methods in Human Geography*, Oxford: Oxford University Press: 19–29.

Duffy, B., K. Hewlett, G. Murkin, R. Benson, R. Hesketh, B. Page et al (2021). *Culture Wars in the UK: Division and Connection*, King's College London and Ipsos.

Duggan, J.R. (2014). 'Critical friendship and critical orphanship: embedded research of an English local authority initiative', *Management in Education* **28**(1): 12–18.

Duncan, S. (2005). *What's the Problem? Teenage Parents: A Critical Review*, London: London South Bank University.

El-Hoss, T., F. Thomas, F. Gradinger and M.S. Hughes (2024). 'Child protection and family support: experiences in a seaside resort', *Geoforum* **148**: art 103943.

Factor, F.J. and E.L. Ackerley (2019). 'Young people and police making "marginal gains": climbing fells, building relationships and changing police safeguarding practice', *Journal of Children's Services* **14**(3): 217–227.

Featherstone, B. and A. Gupta (2018). *Protecting Children: A Social Model,* Bristol: Policy Press.

Ferguson, H. (2014). 'Researching social work practice close up: using ethnographic and mobile methods to understand encounters between social workers, children and families', *The British Journal of Social Work* **46**(1): 153–168.

Firmin, C.E. (2015). *Peer on Peer Abuse: Safeguarding Implications of Contextualising Abuse between Young People within Social Fields,* Luton: University of Bedfordshire.

Firmin, C. (2017a). *Abuse between Young People: A Contextual Account,* Abingdon: Routledge.

Firmin, C. (2017b). *Contextual Safeguarding: An Overview of the Operational, Strategic and Conceptual Framework,* Luton: University of Bedfordshire.

Firmin, C. (2020). *Contextual Safeguarding and Child Protection: Rewriting the Rules,* Abingdon: Routledge.

Firmin, C. (2024). *Risk Outside of the Home Child Protection Pathways: Learning from Phase 2 Pilots,* Durham: Durham University.

Firmin, C. and J. Lloyd (2022). 'Green lights and red flags: the (im)possibilities of contextual safeguarding responses to extra-familial harm in the UK', *Social Sciences* **11**(7): art 303. doi: 10.3390/socsci11070303

Firmin, C., J. Lloyd, J. Walker and R. Owens (2021). 'From "no further action" to taking action: England's shifting social work responses to extra-familial harm', *Critical and Radical Social Work.* doi: 10.1332/204986021X16231574711145

Firmin, C., M. Lefevre, N. Huegler and D. Peace (2022). *Safeguarding Young People beyond the Family Home: Responding to Extra-Familial Risks and Harms,* Bristol: Policy Press.

Firmin, C., L. Wroe and D. Bernard (2022). 'Last resort or best interest? Exploring the risk and safety factors that inform the rates of relocation for young people abused in extra-familial settings', *The British Journal of Social Work* **52**(1): 573–592.

Fischer, F. and G.J. Miller (2017). *Handbook of Public Policy Analysis: Theory, Politics, and Methods,* London: Routledge.

References

Freiberg, A. and W.G. Carson (2010). 'The limits to evidence-based policy: evidence, emotion and criminal justice 1', *Australian Journal of Public Administration* **69**(2): 152–164.

Freud, S. (1940). *Splitting of the Ego in the Process of Defence* (Standard edn, Vol 23, pp 273–278), London: Hogarth.

Fook, J. (2014). Social justice and critical theory. *Routledge International Handbook of Social Justice*, London: Routledge.

Freire, P. (1970). 'Cultural action and conscientization', *Harvard Educational Review* **40**: 452–477.

Frosh, S. (2003). 'Psychosocial studies and psychology: Is a critical approach emerging?', *Human Relations* **56**(12): 1545–1567.

Frost, L. (2019). 'Why psychosocial thinking is critical', in S.A. Webb (ed) *The Routledge Handbook of Critical Social Work*, Abingdon: Routledge: 111–125.

Ghaffar, A., E.V. Langlois, K. Rasanathan, S. Peterson, L. Adedokun and N.T. Tran (2017). 'Strengthening health systems through embedded research', *Bulletin of the World Health Organization* **95**(2): art 87. doi: 10.2471/BLT.16.189126

Gilmore, T.N. (2000). 'Issues in ending consultancies', in R. Golembiewski (ed) *Handbook of Organizational Consultation* (2nd edn), New York: Marcel Dekker: 438–450.

Goodman, S., I. Trowler and E. Munro (2011). *Social Work Reclaimed: Innovative Frameworks for Child and Family Social Work Practice*, London: Jessica Kingsley Publishers.

Guley, G. and T. Reznik (2019). 'Culture eats strategy for breakfast and transformation for lunch', *The Jabian Journal*. Retrieved 7 December 2023, from https://journal.jabian.com/culture-eats-strategy-for-breakfast-and-transformation-for-lunch/

Hall, A.K., A. Oswald, J.R. Frank, T. Dalseg, W.J. Cheung, L. Cooke et al (2024). 'Evaluating Competence by Design as a large system change initiative: readiness, fidelity, and outcomes', *Perspectives on Medical Education* **13**(1): 95–107.

Hallett, S. (2015). '"An uncomfortable comfortableness": "care", child protection and child sexual exploitation', *British Journal of Social Work* **46**(7): 2137–2152.

Hammersley, M. (2006). 'Ethnography: problems and prospects', *Ethnography and Education* **1**(1): 3–14.

Houston, S. (2001). 'Beyond social constructionism: critical realism and social work', *British Journal of Social Work* **31**(6): 845–861.

HM Government (2018). *Working Together to Safeguard Children*, London/Whitehall: Department of Education. Working together to safeguard children – GOV.UK

Hunter, D. and L.E. Wroe (2022). '"Already doing the work": social work, abolition and building the future from the present', *Critical and Radical Social Work*. doi: 10.1332/204986021X16626426254068

Jang, S., T.D. Allen and J. Regina (2021). 'Office housework, burnout, and promotion: does gender matter?' *Journal of Business and Psychology* **36**(5): 793–805.

Jay, A. (2014). *Independent Inquiry into Child Sexual Exploitation in Rotherham: 1997–2013*, Rotherham: Rotherham Metropolitan Borough Council.

Jobe, A. and S. Gorin (2013). '"If kids don't feel safe they don't do anything": young people's views on seeking and receiving help from Children's Social Care Services in England', *Child & Family Social Work* **18**(4): 429–438.

Jones, R.A., N.L. Jimmieson and A. Griffiths (2005). 'The impact of organizational culture and reshaping capabilities on change implementation success: the mediating role of readiness for change', *Journal of Management Studies* **42**(2): 361–386.

Kim, J. (2016). 'Youth involvement in participatory action research (PAR): challenges and barriers', *Critical Social Work* **17**(1): 38–53.

Klein, M. (1952). 'The origins of transference', *International Journal of Psychoanalysis* **33**(4): 433–438.

Knight, R.P. (1940). 'Introjection, projection and identification', *The Psychoanalytic Quarterly* **9**(3): 334–341.

Koshy, V. (2005). *Action Research for Improving Practice: A Practical Guide*, London: Sage.

Lefevre, M., N. Huegler, J. Lloyd, R. Owens, J. Damman, G. Ruch et al (2024). *Innovation in Social Care: New Approaches for Young People Affected by Extra-Familial Risks and Harms*, Bristol: Policy Press.

Lewis, S.J. and A.J. Russell (2011). 'Being embedded: a way forward for ethnographic research', *Ethnography* **12**(3): 398–416.

Lloyd, J. (2019). 'Response and interventions into harmful sexual behaviour in schools', *Child Abuse & Neglect* **94**: art. 104037. doi: 10.1016/j.chiabu.2019.104037

Lloyd, J. (2021). 'Life in a lanyard: developing an ethics of embedded research methods in children's social care', *Journal of Children's Services* **16**(4): 318–331.

Lloyd, J. (2024). *In the Name of Safeguarding: The Education Experiences of Children Experiencing Extra-Familial Harm*, Durham: Durham University.

Lloyd, J. and C. Firmin (2020). 'No further action: contextualising social care decisions for children victimised in extra-familial settings', *Youth Justice* **20**(1–2): 79–92.

Lloyd, J. and R. Owens (2023). 'Developing outcomes measurements in Contextual Safeguarding: explorations of theory and practice', in C. Firmin and J. Lloyd (eds) *Contextual Safeguarding*, Bristol: Policy Press: 147–159.

Lloyd, J., J. Walker and C. Firmin (2020). 'Keeping children safe? Advancing social care assessments to address harmful sexual behaviour in schools', *Child & Family Social Work* **25**(4): 751–760.

Lloyd, J., K. Hickle, R. Owens and D. Peace (2023). 'Relationship-based practice and contextual safeguarding: approaches to working with young people experiencing extra-familial risk and harm', *Children & Society* **38**(4): 1113–1129.

Lloyd, J., M. Manister and L. Wroe (2023). 'Social care responses to children who experience criminal exploitation and violence: the conditions for a welfare response', *The British Journal of Social Work* **53**(8): 3725–3743.

Lloyd, S. (2019). '"She doesn't have to get in the car…": exploring social workers' understandings of sexually exploited girls as agents and choice-makers', *Children's Geographies*. doi: 10.1080/14733285.2019.1649360

Long, S. (2001). 'Working with organizations: the contribution of the psychoanalytic discourse', *Organisational and Social Dynamics* **1**(2): 174–198.

McDowell, L. (1992). 'Doing gender: feminism, feminists and research methods in human geography', *Transactions of the Institute of British Geographers* **17**(4): 399–416.

McGinity, R. and M. Salokangas (2014). 'Introduction: "embedded research" as an approach into academia for emerging researchers', *Management in Education* **28**(1): 3–5.

McIntyre, A. (2007). *Participatory Action Research*, Los Angeles: Sage.

McNamara, P. (2009). 'Feminist ethnography: storytelling that makes a difference', *Qualitative Social Work* **8**(2): 161–177.

Melrose, M. (2013). 'Twenty-first century party people: young people and sexual exploitation in the new millennium', *Child Abuse Review* **22**(3): 155–168.

Menzies, C.R. (2004). 'Putting words into action: negotiating collaborative research in Gitxaala', *Canadian Journal of Native Education* **28**(1–2): 15–32.

Menzies Lyth, I. (1960). 'A case study in the functioning of a social system as a defence against anxiety: a report on the nursing service of a general hospital', *Human Relations* **13**(2): 95–121.

Meyer, J. (2000). 'Using qualitative methods in health related action research', *BMJ* **320**(7228): 178–181.

Millar, H., J. Walker and E. Whittington (2023). 'If you want to help us, you need to hear us', *Contextual Safeguarding*, Bristol: Policy Press: 105–120.

Moore, T. (2006). 'Parallel processes: common features of effective parenting, human services, management and government', keynote address presented at the National Early Childhood Intervention Australia Annual Conference, Melbourne, Australia.

Nijjar, J.S. (2015). '"Menacing youth" and "broken families": A critical discourse analysis of the reporting of the 2011 English riots in the Daily Express using moral panic theory', *Sociological Research Online* **20**(4): 33–44.

Oakley, A. (1993). 'Interviewing women: a contradiction in terms?', in H. Roberts (ed) *Doing Feminist Research*, London: Routledge: 30–61.

Oakley, A. (2016). 'Interviewing women again: power, time and the gift', *Sociology* **50**(1): 195–213.

O'Reilly, K. (2012). *Ethnographic Methods*, London: Routledge.

Ogden, T. (1983). 'The concept of internal object relations', *The International Journal of Psycho-Analysis* **64**: 227.

Owens, R. (2015). 'Working together: using group relations theory to understand and rethink the interplay between administrators and social work practitioners', *Journal of Social Work Practice* **29**(2): 231–238.

Owens, R. (2023). 'Gather round: stories that expand the possibilities of Contextual Safeguarding practice', *Contextual Safeguarding*, Bristol: Policy Press: 175–187.

Owens, R., J. Walker and V. Bradbury-Leather (2024). 'Relational epistemic safety: what young people facing harm in their communities want and need from professionals tasked with helping them', *Journal of Youth Studies*: 1–20.

Owens, R. (2024). *Sustaining Social Work: Practitioner Experiences of Contextual Safeguarding*, Durham: Contextual Safeguarding.

Owens, R. and J. Lloyd (2023). 'From behaviour-based to ecological: multi-agency partnership responses to extra-familial harm', *Journal of Social Work* **23**(4): 741–760.

Ozkazanc-Pan, B. (2012). 'Postcolonial feminist research: challenges and complexities', *Equality, Diversity and Inclusion: An International Journal* **31**(5–6): 573–591.

Parker, S., S. Bennett, C.M. Cobden and D. Earnshaw (2022). '"It's time we invested in stronger borders": media representations of refugees crossing the English Channel by boat', *Critical Discourse Studies* **19**(4): 348–363.

Pearce, J. (2013). 'A social model of "abused consent"', in M. Melrose and J. Pearce (eds) *Critical Perspectives on Child Sexual Exploitation and Related Trafficking*, Basingstoke: Palgrave Macmillan: 52–68.

Phoenix, A. (1988). 'Narrow definitions of culture: the case of early motherhood', in S. Westwood and P. Bhachu (eds) *Enterprising Women: Ethnicity, Economy and Gender Relations*, London: Routledge: 153–176.

Preston-Shoot, M. and D. Agass (1990). Making sense of social work. *Making Sense of Social Work*, Basingstoke: Palgrave Macmillan.

Redman, P. (2016). 'Once more with feeling: What is the psychosocial anyway?', *The Journal of Psychosocial Studies* **9**(1): 73–93.

Reynolds, V. (2011). 'Resisting burnout with justice-doing', *International Journal of Narrative Therapy & Community Work* **4**: 27–45.

Roberts, D. (2021). 'Keynote: how I became a family policing abolitionist', *Columbia Journal of Race and Law* **11**(3): 455–470.

Roulston, K. and M. Choi (2018). 'Qualitative interviews', in U. Flick (ed) *The SAGE Handbook of Qualitative Data Collection*, Los Angeles: Sage: 233–249.

Ruch, G. (2011). 'Where have all the feelings gone? Developing reflective and relationship-based management in child-care social work', *The British Journal of Social Work* **42**(7): 1315–1332.

Ruch, G., I. Julkunen, K. Russell, G. Swann, H. Hingley-Jones, H. Lunabba et al (2016). *Relationship-Based Research in Social Work: Understanding Practice Research*, London: Jessica Kingsley Publishers.

Ruch, G., D. Turney, A. Ward, D. Howe, R. Kohli, M. Smith et al (2018). *Relationship-Based Social Work: Getting to the Heart of Practice* (2nd edn), London: Jessica Kingsley Publishers.

Safer Young Lives (2024). 'Safer young lives research centre'. Retrieved 7 February 2024, from www.beds.ac.uk/sylrc/

Schmich, M. (1997). 'Advice, like youth, probably just wasted on the young', *Chicago Tribune*.

Schön, D.A. (1983). *The Reflective Practitioner: How Professionals Think in Action*, London: Temple Smith.

Schön, D.A. (2017). *The Reflective Practitioner: How Professionals Think in Action*, London: Routledge.

Schram, S.F. and B. Silverman (2012). 'The end of social work: neoliberalizing social policy implementation', *Critical Policy Studies* **6**(2): 128–145.

Scottish Government (2021). *National Guidance for Child Protection in Scotland*, Edinburgh: Scottish Government.

Strier, R. and S. Binyamin (2010). 'Developing anti-oppressive services for the poor: a theoretical and organisational rationale', *British Journal of Social Work* **40**(6): 1908–1926.

Swirak, K. (2016). 'Problematising advanced liberal youth crime prevention: the impacts of management reforms on Irish Garda youth diversion projects', *Youth Justice* **16**(2): 162–180.

Thornhill, L.M. (2023). 'Parents as partners: destigmatising the role of parents of children affected by extra-familial harm', in C. Firmin and J. Lloyd (eds) *Contextual Safeguarding: The Next Chapter*, Bristol: Policy Press: 121–131.

Threlfall-Holmes, M. (2023). 'Question', in K. Venn and M. Wroe (eds) *Fifty: A Festival Lexicon*, London: Greenbelt Festivals: 45–46.

Tobias, J.K., C.A. Richmond and I. Luginaah (2013). 'Community-based participatory research (CBPR) with indigenous communities: producing respectful and reciprocal research', *Journal of Empirical Research on Human Research Ethics* **8**(2): 129–140.

Trevithick, P. (2014). 'Humanising managerialism: reclaiming emotional reasoning, intuition, the relationship, and knowledge and skills in social work', *Journal of Social Work Practice* **28**(3): 287–311.

Ungar, M. (ed) (2021). *Multisystemic Resilience: Adaptation and Transformation in Contexts of Change*, Oxford: Oxford University Press.

Vindrola-Padros, C., T. Pape, M. Utley and N.J. Fulop (2017). 'The role of embedded research in quality improvement: a narrative review', *BMJ Quality & Safety* **26**(1): 70–80.

Vogel, G. (1999). 'Capturing the promise of youth', *Science* **286**(5448): 2238–2239.

Wachtel, T. (1999). 'Restorative justice in everyday life: beyond the formal ritual', Reshaping Australian Institutions Conference: Restorative Justice and Civil Society, The Australian National University, Canberra, Australia.

Wachtel, T. and P. McCold (2004). 'From restorative justice to restorative practices: expanding the paradigm', Fifth International Conference on Conferencing, Circles and Other Restorative Practices, Vancouver, Canada. Retrieved 21 October 2024, from www. realjustice.org/library/bc04_wachtel. html

Waddell, M. (2018). *Inside Lives: Psychoanalysis and the Growth of the Personality*, London: Routledge.

Warrington, C. and C. Larkins (2019). 'Children at the centre of safety: challenging the false juxtaposition of protection and participation', *Journal of Children's Services* **14**(3): 133–142.

Warrington, C., E. Ackerley, H. Beckett and M. Walker (2016). *Making Noise: Children's Voices for Positive Change after Sexual Abuse*, Luton: University of Bedfordshire.

Weiss, C. H. (1995). 'Nothing as practical as good theory: exploring theory-based evaluation for comprehensive community initiatives for children and families', *New Approaches to Evaluating Community Initiatives: Concepts, Methods, and Contexts* **1**: 65–92.

Welsh Government (2020). *Guidance for Education Settings on Peer Sexual Abuse, Exploitation and Harmful Sexual Behaviour*, Cardiff: Welsh Government. Retrieved 19 October 2024, from www.gov.wales/peer-sexual-abuse-exploitation-and-harmful-sexual-behaviour

Westlake, D., L. Stabler and J. McDonnell (2020). 'Direct observation in practice: co-developing an evidence-informed practice tool to assess social work communication', *Journal of Children's Services* **15**(3): 123–140.

Westmarland, N. (2001). 'The quantitative/qualitative debate and feminist research: a subjective view of objectivity', *Forum Qualitative Sozialforschung/Forum Qualitative Social Research* **2**(1). doi: 10.17169/fqs-2.1.974

Williams, J.C. and M. Multhaup (2018). 'For women and minorities to get ahead, managers must assign work fairly', *Harvard Business Review*, 5 March. Retrieved 19 October 2024, from https://hbr.org/2018/03/for-women-and-minorities-to-get-ahead-managers-must-assign-work-fairly

Wilson K., G. Ruch, M. Lymbery and A. Cooper (2008). *Social Work: An Introduction to Contemporary Practice*, Harlow: Pearson.

Winnicott, D.W. (1963). 'The development of the capacity for concern', *Bulletin of the Menninger Clinic* **27**(4): 167–176.

Wong, S. (2009). 'Tales from the frontline: the experiences of early childhood practitioners working with an "embedded" research team', *Evaluation and Program Planning* **32**(2): 99–108.

Woodward, K. (2015). *Psychosocial Studies: An Introduction*, Abingdon: Routledge.

Wroe, L. (2020). 'Principles of Contextual Safeguarding'. Retrieved 1 February 2024, from www.contextualsafeguarding.org.uk/blog/principles-of-contextual-safeguarding/

Wroe, L.E. (2022). 'When helping hurts: a zemiological analysis of a child protection intervention in adolescence–implications for a critical child protection studies', *Social Sciences* **11**(6): 263. doi: 10.3390/socsci11060263

Wroe, L. (2024). *Building Safety: Co-Designing Safety and Fairness into the 'Missing' Response for Young People in Care Who Are at Risk Beyond their Families*, Durham: Durham University.

Wroe, L.E. and J. Lloyd (2020). 'Watching over or working with? Understanding social work innovation in response to extra-familial harm', *Social Sciences* **9**(4): 37. doi: 10.3390/socsci9040037

Wroe, L.E. and M. Manister (2024). 'Relationship of trust and surveillance in the first national piloting of Contextual Safeguarding in England and Wales', *Critical and Radical Social Work* **12**(2): 1–25.

Yardley, L. (2013). 'Introducing material–discursive approaches to health and illness', in L. Yardley (ed) *Material Discourses of Health and Illness*, London: Routledge: 1–24.

Young, T., W. Fitzgibbon and D. Silverstone (2014). 'A question of family? Youth and gangs', *Youth Justice* **14**(2): 171–185.

Index

References to figures appear in *italic* type; those in **bold** type refer to tables.

A

adultification 110, 148
Ahmed, Sara 93
aims 28, 49, 70, 79, 83, 119
assessments 25–6, 28–9, 49
Atkinson, P.E. 108
Auden, W.H. 2
austerity 105, 145
autistic children 53

B

'bad' practice
 feedback 124–9, 129–33, 133–9
 normalising 154
behaviour and environment 109
 sexual behaviour at school 153–4
 social discipline window 133–5, *134*
 see also Contextual Safeguarding
Bhaskar, R. 162
Bigby, C. 110–11, 119–20
Bion, W.R. 101, 161, 166
Black Lives Matter 156–8
Black young people 3, 55
 and 'adultification' 110
blame 167
 victim blaming 53, 82, 109, 113, 148, 161
Bourdieu, P. 3, 108, 109, 139, 160
Bronfenbrenner, U. 3, 109, 161, 169
bullying 83

C

case file reviews 49–56, *54*
CCTV and surveillance 111, 131, 136–7
champions 71, 77, 113–15, 171
change *see* system change

child development 25, 61, 101, 116, 164–5
Children Act 1989 10, 25
children's social care system 6, 27
 child protection response 10–12
 child protection system 25–6
Clarke, S. 3, 164
class 53, 115, 140
Cockbain, E. 12
communication *see* relationships
confidentiality 55
consent 52
consultation 59–62
 with young people 82–4
Contextual Safeguarding 6–7
 about 10–14, 15–17
 adoption of 149
 ending projects 180–4
 framework and values 13–14
 pilot questions 80–1
 pilots 78–9
 system changes 75–82
 see also extra-familial harm; system change
Cooper, A. 101, 177
'county lines' 12
COVID-19 15, 72, 100, 145
 online working 105
crime
 crime prevention 13, 137
 criminal exploitation 12, 32
 drugs 10, 12, 26, 34, 52, 155
 entrenched crime 128, 136
 kidnapping 43
 knife crime 10, 25, 43, 126
 sexual offences 10, 12, 32, 51–3, 131, 187
 shooting 50, 128, 138
critical social work 161

culture 29, 31, 36–7, 50
  about 106–10
  caring culture 116–18
  changing cultures 119–22
  and context 140
  and feedback 127
  normalising 'bad' practice 133, 141
  and professional practice 110–13
  and relationships 113–15
  stories of change 149–58
  understanding culture 56

D

data 5, 32, 57, 66–8
  collection 55, 63, 105, 137, 138, 179
  databases 48–9, 94
death of a child 1, 104, 161
decision-making 31
  based on parenting 51
  influences on 53
  and reasoning 49
defensiveness 125–9, 137, 141, 161, 173
Department of Education 11, 172
developmental needs 25, 61
disability services 120
discursive methods 23, 48–56
drug exploitation 10, 12, 26, 155, 156
drug taking 34, 52
Durham University 14

E

embedded research 8, 14, 72, 164, 168
  and collaboration 47
  doing 56, 60, 62, 123, 166, 171–2
  ending projects 180
  multisystems in *170*
  and relationships 96–8
  what is 4–5
emotions 36, 131–3, 141
  channelling feelings 138–9
  emotional containment 92, 101–3, 161, 166
  and female status 93
  fostering empathy 119–21
  and infants 101
ending projects 180–4
English law 10, 25
environment and change 169
ethics 9
  and observation techniques 38–9
ethnically diverse populations 119, 156, 178

ethnographic methods 23, 29–34
  and embedded research 4
  observation strategies 34–8
  workplace ethnography 39–41
exercises
  aims 28–9
  analytical framework 70
  case file reviews 55
  finding out who you know 99
  getting beneath the service 96
  growing culture 112–13
  mapping 27
  observation templates 33
  relationships of influence 115
  understanding culture 56
external/internal lives 3, 164–5
extra-familial harm 8–9, 10–11, 184
  case file reviews 48–9
  and culture 110, 111, 114, 129
  into policy 13
  Risk Outside the Home 172
  schools approach 83
  system change 75, 78, 80, 152, 155, 165
  understanding 15, 25, 28, 31–2

F

family environment factors 25, 167
family group conferencing 78, 100, 156
Featherstone, B. 163
feedback 59–62, 124–9, 141
  to individuals 135–7
  in system reviews 137–8
feelings *see* emotions
feminist theory 56–7, 93, 162
financial support 167
Firmin, Carlene 10, 11, 14, 65, 149, 155, 169, 172
focus groups 17, 23, 27, 80, 130, 154
Fook, Jan 161
Freud, S. 165
Frost, L. 164, 167, 169
funding 11, 171

G

gangs 55, 120
geographical intervention 79
group relations, 'splitting' 165–6, 173
Gupta, A. 163

H

Hackney, London Borough of 11, 14, 68, 153, 178

Hammersley, M. 4
handover notes 41–4, 66, 103, 159
harm
  significant 10, 25, 50, 51, 78, 126
  structural harm 155–8
Hoggett, P. 3, 164
hospital settings and emotions 101
housing estates 78
housing support 167

I

impact, having an 5, 55, 61–2, 74, 80, 153, 159
implementation 77, 80, 120, 149, 178, 183
Indigenous communities 57
individuals
  individual agency 169
  individualised responsibility 148, 179
  individual pathways 78, 79
inequalities 3, 13, 140, 162, 184
  structural inequalities 3–4, 53, 155, 161, 167–8
intellectual disabilities 110, 119
internal/external lives 3, 164–5
interviews 23, 80

J

Jay, A. 12
judgement 83

K

kidnapping 43
Klein, M. 164–5
knife violence 10, 25, 43, 126
knowledge and world views 170

L

language/terminology 53, 55, 111, 128, 139, 154
Lefevre, M. 12, 99, 117, 147, 158
'like us' approach 120–2
lived experience *see* real life
Lloyd, J. 12, 25, 38, 49, 68, 97, 111, 132, 136, 140, 153, 163
Lloyd, S. 109, 153
local differences 177–80
local leaders 71, 114–15, 119
  relationships with 99–105
locations and safety 78, 150–3
London- based projects 14–17, 72, 177–80

M

mapping the care system 23–7
Marxist thinking 164
McGinity, R. 4, 38, 47, 177
McNamara, P. 163
Melrose, M. 12
Menzies Lyth, I. 3, 57, 101, 161
methodology 6–7, 27–9, 39, 44–8, 161
middle class boys 53
minoritised ethnic groups 119, 156, 178
Moore, T. 116
Multhaup, M. 62
multi-agency meetings 26, 32, 59, 69, 76, 111
multisystemic thinking 168–72
multisystems in embedded research *170*

N

neighbourhoods 11, 78
  parks 13, 131, 156
Nijjar, J.S. 109
notes, writing 36–8
  handover notes 41–4, 66, 103, 159

O

Oakley, Ann 56–7, 162
'object relations' theory 164–5
observation strategies 30–4, 34–8
  and ethics 38–9
  meeting observations 30–1, 80
  observation templates 32–3
Olver, K. 12
online factors
  online harm 13
  sexual imagery 153
  toolkits 7, 149
  working online 105
ordinary, being *see* researchers' working lives
organisations 161
  and emotions 101–2
  and feedback 124–9
  organisational culture 108, 118, 120–1
  and parallel processes 116–18
  and relationships 95–6
'othering' 109–11, 111, 120–1, 166
Owens, R. 80, 83, 125, 132, 146, 149, 158, 163, 184

P

parallel processes 116–18
parenting 10, 12, 25, 154
  the 'bad' parent 166–7
  consulting with parents 82–4
  and context 50
parks 13, 78, 131, 156
partnerships 13, 67
peer groups 11, 78, 152
perspectives 44, 64, 83, 106, 135, 160
pilots 75–81, 85
  pilot questions 80–1
planning meetings 26, 80, 82–4
see also system change
police 26, 32, 43, 52, 59, 71, 117, 156
  and information sharing 130, 136
  police-centred approach 36
  police-led responses 139
  and racism 3
positionality 106, 134
positive, being 68, 112, 120, 130, 136
  recording moments of 159
positivist research 60, 169
poverty 136, 161, 167
  intergenerational poverty 179
power dynamics 31, 56–7, 97, 109
  power sharing **58**
  and young people 110
professionals'
  'bad' practice in context
    139–40, 154
  and change 148
  concerns of 42–3
  and culture 110–13
  derogatory language 111–12
  and feedback 124–9
  and racism 156–8
  relationships with 9, 55, 79, 92–9
  staff turnover 179–80
  and structural issues 166, 167
  and victim blaming 109
psychosocial approaches 7, 92, 161, 168–9
  emotional containment 101–3
  and understanding systems 162–8
public policy changes 12

R

racism 3, 53, 140, 148, 155–8, 170
rape 12, 51–3
real life 2, 146, 162
  and embedded research 4–5
real-life approach 177
real-life change 2–4, 14, 163–4
reciprocal methods 23, 56–62, 57, 63
reflection 166–7, 168
reflective meetings 66–70, 106, 129, 141
reflective support 173
regional differences 177–80
relationships 63, 92–9, 172
  being 'good enough' 103–5
  building relationships 99–105
  and culture 107, 113–15
  embedded relationality 105–6
  and embedded research 4–5
  and emotions 101–3
  and feedback 126
  relational approach 47, 140, 163
  trusting relationships 55–7, 96, 129
researchers' working lives 1–2, 39, 46–7, 71–3
  being 'good enough' 103–6
  being 'ordinary' 57, 60, 63, 97
  clothing 178–9
  consultation 59–62
  and emotions 123–4, 131–3
  ending projects 180–4
  online working 105
  and power 56
  wellbeing 67
  see also relationships
residential care homes, culture in 110–11, 119
restorative practice 134–5
rights-based approach 13, 84, 111, 179
Risk Outside the Home 172
risky behaviours 131, 140
Ruch, G. 93, 102, 161

S

safeguarding 6, 11–13
  children's social care 27–8
  culture of 111
  failures 50, 133
  referrals and assessments 25–6
  in schools 153
  see also Contextual Safeguarding
safety
  and locations 150–3
  safer streets 10, 120, 135
  safer swimming 151–2
  safe spaces 83, 102
Salokangas, M. 4, 38, 47, 177

Scale-Up project 8, 14–17, 49, 65, 72, 75, 178
  ending projects 180–4
  language and terminology 113
  online toolkit 9, 149, 184
school 11, 13, 26, 71, 78, 119
  exclusion 36–7, 156, 184
  non-attendance 155
  school assessments 78
  sexual behaviour 153–4
  whole school approach 83
sexism 148
sexual abuse 52–3
sexual assault 87, 131
sexual behaviour at school 153–4
sexual exploitation 10, 12, 32
shame 58, 130, 167
shootings 50, 128, 138
single point of contact (SPOC) 17, 73, 104, 106
  and caring culture 116–18
  and case reviews 48–9
  and cultural change 107
  ending projects 181–2
  language and terminology 113–15
  and racism 157–8
  relationships with 92, 99–105
social care system, mapping the 23–7
social construction theories 163
social discipline window 133–5, *134*
social norms and behaviour 133
sociological approaches 3, 7, 160
strengths-based approach 13
structural harm 155–8
structural inequality 3–4, 53, 155, 161, 167–8
structural racism 158
suicide 138
surveillance 111, 131, 136–7
swimming in rivers 151–2
system change 6–8, 11–13, 22–4, 44, 159, 176–7
  and applied research 17
  'bad' practice feedback 124–9
  as a complex process 185
  and Contextual Safeguarding 75–82
  and emotions 102
  ending projects 180–4
  incremental change 147–9

making a plan 64–5
and organisational culture 108
regional differences 177–80
stories of 149–58
system change plans 73–5, 76–7, **76**, 84–5
system change theory 169–70
and systemic harm 155–8
system review process 65–71
and theories 160–2
understanding systems 162–8
see also culture; feedback; relationships
systemic issues 148
systemic racism 156
systemic violence 124, 155–8

T

theories
  multisystemic thinking 168–72
  psychosocial concepts 162–8
  and system change 160–2
Thornhill, L.M. 12, 82, 184
threshold for social care 12, 49
Tobias, J.K. 57
traffic light tool 68–9, **69**
training 61, 71, 79, 138
Trevithick, P. 93, 118

U

United Kingdom 10
  political and social environment 145
  projects in 177, 182
University of Bedfordshire 9, 14

V

values 13–14, 108, 109, 120, 130
vaping 117
victim blaming 53, 82, 109, 113, 148, 161
violence 10
  and abuse 50
  sexual offences 12, 32, 51–3, 87, 131
  street violence 10
Vogel, G. 109
voluntary/community sector 16, 49, 82, 154, 165

W

Wachtel, T. 133–4
Weiss, C.H. 169
welfare responses 67
Williams, J.C. 62

Wilson, K.G. 169
Winnicott, D.W. 103
women
 and emotions 93
 research interviews 56–7
 in the workplace 62
 workforce stability 179
 Working Together to Safeguard Children 25, 149
workshops 82, 136
Wroe, L. 11, 13, 111, 131, 136, 140, 149, 155

Y

Yardley, L. 48
Young, T. 120
young people
 attitudes towards 109–11, 120–1, 128, 130, 154–5
 consulting with 82–4
 exploitation of 10, 12, 26, 32, 155
 and extra-familial harm 8–9
 from minoritised backgrounds 119
 safer spaces for 135

www.ingramcontent.com/pod-product-compliance
Lightning Source LLC
Chambersburg PA
CBHW051542020426
42333CB00016B/2061